Vocabulary Mastery 3

Using and Learning the Academic Word List

LINDA WELLS
GLADYS VALCOURT

Ann Arbor
The University of Michigan Press

Published in the United States of America
The University of Michigan Press
Manufactured in the United States of America

∞ Printed on acid-free paper

ISBN-13: 978-0-472-03314-0

2013 2012 2011 2010 4 3 2 1

Acknowledgments

Many thanks to Lida Baker, Cheryl Delk, Robyn Brinks Lockwood, and Mary Ann Maynard for their contributions to these units and the final product.

Grateful acknowledgment is given to the following authors, publishers, and individuals for permission to reprint their materials or previously published materials.

AWL List

Permission granted by Averil Coxhead to use the Academic Word List in Appendix 1 and in the book's subtitle.

Unit 1

Unit-opening photo (the Guggenheim) courtesy of Jupiter Unlimited.

Adapted excerpts from *Many Masks: The Life of Frank Lloyd Wright* by Brendan Gill, published with permission of Putnam, 1987.

Adapted excerpts from *Frank Lloyd Wright: An Autobiography,* published by Pomegranate Communications, 1943.

Photo of the Imperial Hotel courtesy The Frank Lloyd Wright Archives in Scottsdale, Arizona.

Photo of Fallingwater courtesy The Frank Lloyd Wright Archives in Scottsdale, Arizona.

Photo of Taliesin courtesy The Frank Lloyd Wright Foundation, Arizona/Art Resource, NY.

Unit 2

Unit-opening photo courtesy of Jupiter Unlimited.

Adapted excerpts from *Personal History* by Katharine Graham, published by Knopf, 1997. Used by permission of Alfred A. Knopf, a division of Random House.

Excerpt from *The Secret Man: The Story of Watergate's Deep Throat* by Bob Woodward, published by Simon Schuster. Copyright 2005 Bob Woodward. Used with permission.

Photo still from *All the President's Men* courtesy the Museum of Modern Art.

Political cartoon of Richard M. Nixon on page 42 courtesy the Library of Congress.

Photo of W. Mark Felt courtesy of Wikipedia.

Unit 3

Unit-opening photo and photo on page 66 of Mt. Everest and photos of marathon on page 69 and runner on page 69 courtesy of Jupiter Unlimited.

Adapted excerpts from *Into Thin Air: A Personal Account of the Mt. Everest Disaster* by John Krakauer, copyright 1997 by Jon Krakauer. Used by permission of Anchor, a division of Random House.

Excerpt from *What I Talk about When I Talk about Running: A Memoir* by Haruki Murakami, translated by Philip Gabriel, translation copyright © 2008 by Haruki Murakami. Used by permission of Alfred A. Knopf, a division of Random House.

Reading about a triathalon adapted from www.active.com/triathalon/Articles/2008_Accenture_Chicago_Triathalon_Race-Review.html.

Unit 4

Unit-opening photo courtesy of Jupiter Unlimited.

Adapted excerpts from *Mockingbird: A Portrait of Harper Lee* by Charles J. Shields, published by Henry Holt, 2006.

Photos from the set of *To Kill a Mockingbird* courtesy of MPTV Images. Used with permission.

Unit 5

Unit-opening photo and photo on page 125 courtesy of Jupiter Unlimited.

Excerpts updated from *Preventing Emerging Infectious Diseases: A Strategy for the 21st Century,* published by the Centers for Disease Control, 1998.

Excerpt from *Voice of America* report "WHO Calls for Urgent Action Against Multidrug—Resistant TB in Asia-Pacific," 2007.

Excerpt from the Centers for Disease Control Division of Tuberculosis, 2009.

Data from the World Health Organization used to compile the figure on page 123.

Unit 6

Unit-opening photo of Sequoia National Forest, Old Faithful, and Teddy Roosevelt courtesy of Jupiter Unlimited.

Adapted excerpts from the National Park Service website www.nps.gov/history/.

Excerpt from *From Walden to Wall Street: Frontiers of Conservation Finance,* edited by James N. Levitt, published by Island Press. Copyright 2005 by Lincoln Institute of Land Policy. Used with permission.

Every effort has been made to contact the copyright holders for permission to reprint borrowed material. We regret any oversights that may have occurred and will rectify them in future printings of this book.

Contents

To the Teacher

Teachers and students alike realize that strong vocabulary skills are necessary for academic success. Specifically, students need to know the vocabulary they will most frequently encounter in their academic studies in order to successfully complete their reading and writing assignments. The *Vocabulary Mastery* series teaches students the words they need to know to succeed in their academic work. These words come from the Academic Word List (AWL) developed by Averill Coxhead ["A New Academic Word List," *TESOL Quarterly* 34, no. 2 (2000): 213–38]. The Academic Word List resulted from Coxhead's analysis of a broad corpus of academic texts—about 3.5 million words—from 414 academic texts in 28 topic areas. Out of this corpus, Coxhead selected the 570 word families that occur most frequently in academic texts. *Vocabulary Mastery* teaches these word families.

Learning vocabulary involves more than simply recognizing a word. In order to truly know a word, students must:

- **Have multiple exposures to the word.** Nation [*Teaching and Learning Vocabulary*, Newbury House, 1990] concluded that a word needs to be encountered anywhere from five to more than 16 times before it is learned. The readings and exercises in *Vocabulary Mastery* provide students with multiple exposures to the target vocabulary. Activities that require students to do outside reading also increase their exposure to the target vocabulary.
- **Know more than the meaning, spelling, and pronunciation of a word.** Students must also learn the grammar of the word, the words it frequently occurs or collocates with, the associations a word has, the frequency with which it occurs, and its register. *Vocabulary Mastery* uses an effective interactive approach that develops both explicit and implicit word knowledge. The exercises in this book provide students with word knowledge that is explicitly taught (spelling, meaning, pronunciation, and collocation). It also provides numerous encounters with words to help students develop their own implicit, contextual knowledge (association and register) of words.
- **Be familiar with other members of a word's family.** By learning some or all of a word family, students are able to use the correct form of a word within a particular context. Every unit in *Vocabulary Mastery* contains exercises that focus on word families and derivations.
- **Understand collocations.** Knowledge of collocations makes word use more natural. Exercises in *Vocabulary Mastery* teach some of the more common collocations of the target vocabulary. More important, though,

these exercises raise students' awareness of collocations, which may help students notice collocations when they occur and build their own knowledge of collocation.

- **Know that one word can have different meanings used in different contexts.** Exercises show the different meanings of a target word in the appropriate contexts. Students are encouraged to use a dictionary to help them learn these different meanings.
- **Learn to focus on the words they want to learn.** The readings and exercises in *Vocabulary Mastery 3* contain more than 300 words from the AWL, more than in *Vocabulary Mastery 1* and *2*. To aid students in learning, the target vocabulary in the readings is marked in **bold.** Other AWL vocabulary items (any form of the item) in the readings are underlined. Words and idioms that occur infrequently but are needed to understand the text are glossed in the margins. Appendix 1 is an excellent resource for revealing just how many academic words students are learning in this volume and in this series; it also shows that many words in this book are reinforced and repeated.

The readings and vocabulary appear in an order so that skills and concepts are built upon as students progress through the book.

In addition to academic vocabulary, this text helps students develop the critical-thinking skills necessary for academic achievement. Activities in each unit require students to think about and analyze what they have read. In addition, writing assignments require students to think critically about what they have read as they learn and practice skills they will need in their academic classes. These skills include answering questions and supporting answers with concrete examples, interpreting a chart and answering questions about it, ordering information chronologically and writing paragraphs that give that information, analyzing and writing about a problem they select, summarizing, giving an opinion, and identifying causes and effects.

Vocabulary Mastery 3 has six units, each on a particular high-interest theme. Each of the six units is divided into

- **Vocabulary Preview 1 and 2.** These exercises help students and teachers discover how much target vocabulary is already familiar.
- **Reading Preview.** These questions are designed to activate students' prior knowledge of the topic.
- **Introduction to the Readings.** An introductory reading about the topic provides background information about the readings that follow.
- **Two or three readings of various lengths on a theme or topic that contain 15 target words from the Academic Word List.** In most units, at least one reading is biographical or autobiographical, and the other

readings are from other non-fiction sources. In the final two units, all the readings are non-fiction and come from more complex and more difficult original sources. Students will notice that as this book progresses, the number of words in readings from the Academic Word List increases. This reveals just how frequent these words are to academic content, especially non-fiction. The variety of readings exposes students to the target words in different writing styles and voices. In addition to the target vocabulary, all of the readings expose students to a number of other words and their word forms from the AWL and recycle AWL words already learned.

- **Comprehension Check.** This series of True/False questions determines how well students understood the Introduction and Readings.
- **A list of 15 target vocabulary words from the Academic Word List.**
- **At least ten vocabulary-based activities that include**
  - ➢ Understanding Words
    - —Word Parts: suffixes, prefixes, and roots
    - —Word Relationships: synonyms, antonyms, collocations, and analogies
    - —Word Families Chart: a target word and its most commonly used derivatives
    - —Word Forms and Derivatives
    - —Commonly Confused Words
  - ➢ Understanding Words in Context
    - —Using Words Correctly
    - —Making Inferences
    - —Constructing Sentences
    - —Word Meanings: multiple or similar meanings of a word
    - —Context Clues/Meanings in Context
  - ➢ Using Words in Communication
    - —Reading activities that encourage research and outside reading about the topic
    - —Writing activities that ask students to react, summarize, and give an opinion
  - ➢ Critical-Thinking Tasks
    - —Questions and tasks to be used for writing assignments or class discussion

The exercises and activities in *Vocabulary Mastery 3* give students the opportunity to study academic vocabulary in two important ways: Students encounter each word as a discrete language unit and also within natural contexts as part of a whole language system.

We hope that you and your students find this textbook is a useful and enjoyable way to learn vocabulary from the Academic Word List. Good luck in your endeavors!

To the Student

Vocabulary Mastery 3 will help you learn the vocabulary words that you will need to know to do well in your academic studies. These words come from the Academic Word List (Coxhead 2000), which contains 570 words common in the variety of academic reading texts you will encounter. These words may be different from the words you hear and use in your everyday life. By learning these words with a basic 2,000-word vocabulary, you will be able to understand more than 85 percent of academic reading assignments. Some suggestions for using this text follow. Your teacher may have others.

1. Find out how much vocabulary you already know by doing the **Vocabulary Preview** exercises in each unit.
2. Review words in the **Word Study** section. Cross out words that you already know.
3. Use your dictionary to find the meanings of words you do not know. Write these in a vocabulary notebook or make vocabulary cards (see How to Make Vocabulary Cards on page xiii). When you finish this textbook, you will have your own reference of academic vocabulary.
4. Read the introduction and readings in the unit. Check your dictionary for words that are not listed on your vocabulary list that you need to know to understand the reading.
5. As you read, check to see whether you understand what you are reading. Ask yourself: Did I understand what I just read? Which sentence or word is giving me a problem? Why? What or who can help me understand this? Can I ask a classmate or my teacher to help me?
6. Answer the **Comprehension Check** questions, which will show you how well you have understood the introduction and readings. The questions here are answered with True or False. If you have trouble, you may want to reread the introduction and readings.
7. Once you think that you understand the introduction and readings, complete the activities in the **Word Study** section.
8. When you have finished all of the **Word Study** activities, check your answers in the online key, if your teacher says it's okay.
9. Reread the introduction and readings. Have they become easier to understand?

10. Use outside materials such as books, magazine articles, videos, and films to help you learn more about the topic in each unit. Your local library and the Internet are good places to find outside material.

Completing this textbook will help you to learn the words you need for academic success. Good luck in your studies!

How to Make Vocabulary Cards

Vocabulary cards are an easy way to study and review new vocabulary words. Make your own vocabulary cards by following these directions.

1. Use one card for each word. You can buy inexpensive index cards at most supermarkets or drugstores.
2. Write each vocabulary word on the front of a card.
3. Write the meaning or meanings of each word on the back of the card in English. You might also want to write the meaning in your native language if you are learning English.
4. Add other helpful information on the back of the card. You might want to include:
   - how the word is pronounced
   - an example sentence for the word
   - a picture that helps you remember the meaning of the word
   - other members of the word's family
   - words that collocate or often appear with that vocabulary word
5. Keep your cards in a box or put them on a ring. Practice with the cards for a few minutes every day. Look at the word on the front of the card, and see if you can remember its meaning. Check the definition on the back of the card to see if you are correct.
6. When you know a word well, move the card to the back of the box. If you don't know a word, keep it near the front to practice it often.
7. Review the vocabulary words frequently. This will help you remember and master these important academic vocabulary words.

1 Architecture

Vocabulary Preview

Preview 1

These sentences contain information from the readings. Fill in the blanks with the word that best completes each sentence.

adjacent **assist** **distortion** **infrastructure** **utilized**

1. One of Frank Lloyd Wright's most famous houses, *Fallingwater*, was built ____________ to a stream.

2. The ____________ of the Imperial Hotel consisted of short concrete "fingers" resting on sixty feet of mud.

3. Frank Lloyd Wright ____________ natural materials such as stone and wood to build homes in several Midwestern American cities.

4. In Japan, building materials must be both strong and flexible to prevent ____________ of structures during an earthquake.

5. Wright's home included living space for young workers who came to ____________ him in his work.

Preview 2

Look at the way the underlined words are used in the sentences. Match each word with its meaning or definition.

1. Wright designed his home for himself, his children, and for many future generations.

2. After inspecting Wright's design for his house, Edgar Kaufmann expressed disappointment that it would not have a view of the waterfall.

3. The owners of Fallingwater took great pleasure in the house's location and appearance. Nevertheless, they were never sure the house was safe.

4. Wright designed many unusual commercial buildings, but his famous "Prairie Homes," built in several Midwestern cities, are even more innovative.

5. Over time, the great weight of the Imperial Hotel caused the concrete foundation to sink as much as four feet.

_____	1. **generations**	a. however
_____	2. **inspecting**	b. underlying base for a building, usually made of concrete
_____	3. **nevertheless**	c. all the people of about the same age in a society or family
_____	4. **innovative**	d. examining closely
_____	5. **foundation**	e. new and unusual

Reading Preview: What Do You Already Know?

Circle the correct answer. If you don't know the answer, guess.

1. Frank Lloyd Wright is a famous
   a. architect
   b. inventor
   c. author

2. Frank Lloyd Wright lived from
   a. 1867 to 1951
   b. 1900 to 1973
   c. 1920 to 1990

3. The Imperial Hotel was most famous for
   a. having a steel foundation
   b. surviving a great earthquake
   c. introducing Native American decorating themes to Japan

4. The house Wright named Fallingwater is most famous for
   a. being built over a waterfall
   b. falling into the river after it was completed
   c. being designed to look like a waterfall

5. Wright designed all of these buildings except
   a. Taliesin West
   b. Westcott House
   c. Bear House

Introduction to the Readings

(1) Frank Lloyd Wright, born in 1867 in Richland Center, Wisconsin, created a truly unique, modern, American style of architecture. His buildings are known for their dramatic, clean lines and often unusual settings. Although Wright designed many **innovative** commercial buildings, his "Prairie Homes," built in several Midwestern American cities, are equally famous. Wright's prolific* and ground-breaking career spanned 70 years and included 1,000 designs and more than 500 completed projects.

*__prolific:__ productive, creating a lot of work

(2) Readings 1 and 3 are adapted from Brendan Gill's *Many Masks: A Life of Frank Lloyd Wright* and discuss two of Wright's most famous buildings: the Tokyo Imperial Hotel in Japan and the unique "Fallingwater" house in Bear Run, Pennsylvania.

(3) Reading 2 comes from Wright's autobiography. It describes how his beloved home, Taliesin, came to be and provides a look into how personal this design was to Wright. Taliesin was rebuilt more than once due to fires and eventually was used mostly for training of new architects. The house still stands today, as does Taliesin West, which Wright built in Scottsdale, Arizona, in 1937. Fallingwater was designed while Wright lived at Taliesin.

Reading 1: The Imperial Hotel

Excerpt adapted from *The Many Masks of Frank Lloyd Wright* by Brendan Gill (New York: Putnam, 1987), pp. 257–64.

(4) The Imperial Hotel, built in Tokyo in 1922 and eventually torn down in 1967, was one of Wright's most significant works. The chief fame of the Imperial Hotel comes from its having survived the great earthquake of 1923, but the hotel was also known for its vast public spaces, unusual **infrastructure,** and stark* interior decoration. The Mayan themes, which had been evident themselves in some of Wright's earlier buildings, were done beautifully in local stone.

*__stark:__ not cheerful, empty

The Imperial Hotel. Photo courtesy The Frank Lloyd Wright Archives, Scottsdale, AZ.

(5) From the beginning, Wright was aware that earthquakes were common in Japan. In his designs for the hotel, he would have to confront what he described as "this terrible natural enemy of all buildings—the tremblor." In his autobiography he wrote: "For more than four years, I worked upon it . . . I studied the tremblor. I found it a wave-movement, not of sea, but of earth. Because of the wave movements, deep **foundations** like long piles would oscillate* and rock the **structure.** There were 60 or 70 feet of soft mud below the eight feet of surface soil. The mud seemed a good cushion to relieve the terrible shocks. Why not float the building upon it? Why not a building made like two hands thrust together palms inward, fingers, interlocking and yielding to movement—but resilient* enough to return to its original position when the **distortion** ceased?

***oscillate:** move up and down or side to side

***resilient:** able to withstand change

(6) With the **assistance** of builder Paul Mueller, Wright set about floating his vast **structure** on a couple of thousand short, close-set concrete "fingers." Wright's protégé, Antonin Raymond, claimed that the fingers never really worked and that what Mueller and Wright ended up with was an immense concrete slab resting on mud. Regardless of the truth, the project continued year after year, with Wright constantly changing his plans according to the capacities of the indigenous* Japanese workforce and his ever-increasing knowledge of what the hotel would need to have in order to serve both its foreign and Japanese clients.

***indigenous:** native to or born in

(7) Though the hotel was not yet finished, Wright left Tokyo for the last time in 1921. The famous sequel to the story about the building of the Imperial Hotel came two years later when Tokyo and Yokohama suffered devastation in the greatest earthquake in Japanese history. The Imperial Hotel suffered some comparatively minor damage. However, what is more important to history is that an overwhelming majority of the steel-framed buildings in Tokyo easily survived the earthquake and that Wright's "floating" **foundation** was no more successful in resisting the earthquake than the conventional **foundations** of other steel-framed buildings. Moreover, through the years, the great weight of the hotel caused it to subside, or sink, continuously on its unstable concrete **foundation**, in some places to a depth of four feet. The high cost of maintaining the basic **utilities** of the hotel in the face of this subsidence was one of the chief reasons for its demolition in 1967. The hotel was gorgeous, but it was by no means the engineering marvel* that Wright said it was.

***marvel:** masterpiece

Reading 2: Taliesin

Excerpt adapted from *Frank Lloyd Wright: An Autobiography,* (San Franscisco: Pomegranate Communications, 1943). 167–71.

(8) Taliesin was the name of a Welsh poet, a druid* who sang to Wales about the glories of fine art. Since all my relatives had Welsh names for their places, why not Taliesin for mine? Literally the Welsh word means "shining brow."

***druid:** member of a pre-Christian religious group

(9) This hill on which Taliesin now stands as "brow" was one of my favorite places. As a boy I had learned to know the plan of the region in every line and feature. I still feel myself as much a part of it as the trees and birds and bees are, and the red barns. Or as the animals are, for that matter.

(10) It was unthinkable to me, at least unbearable, that any house should be put *on* that beloved hill. I knew well no house should ever be *on* a hill or *on* anything. It should be *of* the hill. Belonging to it. Hill and house should live together each the happier for the other. Now I wanted a *natural* house to live in myself. I scanned the hills of the region where the rock came cropping out in strata* to suggest buildings. How quiet and strong the rock-ledge masses looked with the dark red cedars and white birches . . . above the green slopes. They were all part of southern Wisconsin.

***strata (stratum):** layers or levels

(11) I wished to be part of my beloved southern Wisconsin, too. . . . There must be some kind of house that would belong to that hill, as trees and the ledges of rock did. . . . There must be a natural house, not natural as caves and log-cabins were natural, but native in spirit and the making, having itself all that architecture had meant whenever it was alive in times past. Nothing that I had ever seen would work. Yes, there was a house that hill might marry and live happily with ever after. I fully intended to find it. I even saw for myself what it might be like. And I began to build it as the brow of that hill. . . .

Taliesin, 1914–1925, Spring Green, WI. View from the hill garden. Photo by Henry Fuermann, 1915. Photo courtesy the Frank Lloyd Wright Foundation, AZ/Art Resource, NY.

(12) Taliesin, of course, was to be an architect's workshop, a dwelling as well, for young workers who would come to **assist.** And it was a farm cottage for the farm help. Around the rear were to be farm buildings, for Taliesin was to be a complete living unit genuine in point of comfort and beauty. . . . The place was to be self-<u>sustaining</u> if not self-<u>sufficient</u>, and with its <u>domain</u> of two hundred acres was to be shelter, food, clothes, and even entertainment within itself. It had to be its own light—plant, fuel yard, <u>transportation,</u> and water system.

(13) Taliesin was to be recreation ground for my children and their children, perhaps for many **generations** more. This modest human program in terms of rural Wisconsin arranged itself around the hilltop in a <u>series</u> of four <u>varied</u> courts leading one into the other, the courts all together forming a sort of drive along the hillside, with low buildings on one side and flower gardens against the stone walls that <u>retained</u> the hill on the other.

(14) The hill-crown was thus saved and the buildings became a brow for the hill itself. . . . Taliesin was to be an abstract combination of stone and wood as they naturally met in the aspect of the hills. And the lines of the hills were the lines of the roofs, the slopes of the hills their slopes, the plastered surfaces of the light wood-walls, set back into shade beneath broad eaves, were like the flat stretches of sand in the river below and the same in color, for that is where the material that covered them came from. . . .

(15) When all was clean and in place, Taliesen beamed; it wore a happy smile of well-being and welcome for all.

(16) It was intensely human, I believe.

Reading 3: Fallingwater

Excerpt adapted from *The Many Masks of Frank Lloyd Wright* by Brendan Gill (New York: Putnam, 1987), pp. 343–54.

(17) In 1934, a young man of 24 named Edgar J. Kaufmann, Jr., asked Wright to design an all-year-round country house for a beautiful piece of wilderness property on a stream called Bear Run, in the mountains about 60 miles south of Pittsburgh, Pennsylvania. Wright visited the site and noted, among other things, a very large and smooth boulder overhanging the waterfall that was Bear Run's most remarkable feature. A map of the site was sent to Wright during the winter of 1935, along with word that the Bear Run house should be planned to cost between $20,000 and $30,000.

(18) To Kaufmann's distress, many weeks passed and no drawings or plans arrived from Wright's workshop in Taliesin, Wisconsin. Finally, Kaufman's father, on business in the Midwest, decided to visit Taliesin himself. Little did he know that Wright had not yet drawn a single line on the Bear Run project. When Wright heard that Kaufmann was coming, according to one of his **assistants,** he "sat down at the table . . . and started to draw. First floor. Second floor. Section, elevation. The design just poured out of him. Pencils were used

Fallingwater. Photo courtesy The Frank Lloyd Wright Archives, Scottsdale, AZ.

up as fast as they could be sharpened. Erasures, overdrawing, modifying. Then, Wright added the bold title across the bottom: 'Fallingwater.' The name simply, and delightfully, reversed the word *waterfall*. . . .

(19) "Just before noon, Mr. Kaufmann [Sr.] arrived. He was greeted graciously by the master. . . . Then the description of the house, its setting, its **philosophy** poured out. . . . [From that moment,] the basic design never changed."

(20) Fallingwater is an astonishing house. It stands, or appears to stand, upon air. Projecting out over Bear Run by means of an almost invisible concrete supports, the house and its terraces seem to float above the waterfall. Wright said of the house, "I think you can hear the waterfall when you look at the design." The only mild objection that Kaufmann raised to the unusual **structure** after **inspecting** the design was that he had thought the house would be located on the opposite side, **adjacent** to Bear Run, where it would

offer a pleasing view of the waterfall. Wright made no effort to disguise the fact that the house, as he had designed it, was in the one place where it would be impossible to view the waterfall. On the **contrary,** he emphasized the peculiarity, saying, "I want you to live with the waterfall, not just look at it."

(21) Edgar Kaufmann has written that "it was an extraordinary moment when the full force of Wright's concept became apparent. We did not hesitate—whatever the previous expectations and whatever the problems suggested by the plans." The **prospects** were exhilarating."

(22) The risks assumed in the siting and construction of Fallingwater were more than justified by its appearance and by the pleasure the Kaufmanns and their guests took in the house. **Nevertheless,** the risks were real, and Kaufmann himself never felt sure that the building was safe. Cracks would appear in the concrete and be mended and reappear; deflections of the cantilevered terraces could be seen by the naked eye, though most of them were minor and were caused by changes in temperature from season to season. Kaufmann was impatient with the idea that the **structure's** flaws amounted to a serious criticism of Wright's planning. He writes, "The architect and his client knew the design of Fallingwater was an exploration beyond the limits of conventional practice." Some of the great monuments of architecture have suffered **structural** troubles, precisely because they were striving beyond normal limitations. Yet these buildings still stand and add glory to their countries and their art. My father was no monarch and his house is not a public monument, but Wright's genius justifies these references. No apologies are necessary for what Wright **achieved** at Fallingwater."

Comprehension Check

Did you understand the readings? Mark these sentences true (T) or false (F).

_____ 1. The Tokyo Imperial Hotel stood for less than 50 years.

_____ 2. Wright used Mayan themes for the first time in his design for the Imperial Hotel.

_____ 3. By the time the hotel was completed, Wright had already left Japan.

_____ 4. In the earthquake of 1923, the Imperial Hotel was damaged less badly than conventional steel-framed buildings.

_____ 5. Like his relatives, Wright wanted to give his own house a Welsh name.

_____ 6. For Wright, the most important thing about Taliesin was that it should be located on top of a hill.

_____ 7. Taliesin was a combination workshop, family home, and farm cottage.

_____ 8. Taliesin was built out of bricks, concrete, and bamboo.

_____ 9. The first house that Wright designed for Edgar Kaufmann was called Bear Run.

_____ 10. The house appears to float above a waterfall.

_____ 11. Structurally, the house was perfect.

_____ 12. Both Wright and Kaufmann knew that the house was unusual for its time.

Word Study

Target Vocabulary

achieve
adjacent
assist (assistance)
contrary
distort (distortion)
foundation
generation
infrastructure
innovate (innovative)
inspect
nevertheless
philosophy
prospect
structure
utilize (utilities)

Word Parts

English words that originally came from Latin or Greek often have three parts: a prefix, a root, and a suffix. The **root** is the part of the word that carries the basic meaning. A **prefix** is a syllable that is added before the root to give it a new meaning. A **suffix** is a syllable added after the root that determines the grammar of the word. Words may have a prefix and a root, a root and a suffix, or all three parts.

Take, for example, the word *philosophy:*

	phil(o)	soph	y
Word part	prefix	root	suffix
Meaning	love	wisdom	noun

Thus, *philosophy* originally meant "the love of wisdom."

Exercise 1: Roots

The root *-struct-* means "building." Study the chart of prefixes and suffixes that combine with *-struct-*. Form the words that match the definitions using a combination of prefixes and/or suffixes, and write them on the lines. (Notes: Verbs will not have suffixes. Words can have more than one prefix.)

Prefix	Root	Suffix
con- meaning "with"	*-struct-*	*-tion* meaning "the act of"
de- meaning "take away"	*-struct-*	*-tion* meaning "the act of"
in- meaning "in"	*-struct-*	*-tion* meaning "the act of"
infra- meaning "down, under"	*-struct-*	*-ure* meaning "result/action"
re- meaning "again"	*-struct-*	*-ure* meaning "result/action"

1. ________________ to build in knowledge; to teach

2. ________________ the act of building something, such as a home or road

3. ________________ the foundation of a building, bridge, etc.

4. ________________ the act of taking something apart or tearing down

5. ________________ to build something again after it has been destroyed or taken apart

Can you think of other words formed with the root *–struct-*? Write them here. Compare with a classmate.

________________ ________________ ________________

Exercise 2: Suffixes

There are many noun suffixes in English. Look at five examples.

-ation	-ance	-ment	-ity	-al[1]
foundation	acceptance	environment	university	removal

Of these suffixes, the most common one is *-tion.*

Add noun suffixes to these words and roots. Follow the spelling rules for adding suffixes. If necessary, use a dictionary to check your answers.

1. achieve______
2. assist______
3. distort______
4. inspect ______
5. creative ______
6. transport______
7. vary_______
8. survive_____

Write one sentence using each of the nouns you formed.

[1] This suffix sometimes marks an adjective, as in *normal.*

Word Relationships

Synonyms are words that have similar meanings. For example, synonyms for *normal* include *typical, regular, usual, average,* and *standard.* **Antonyms** are words that have opposite meanings. Antonyms for *significant* include *unimportant, trivial, meaningless,* and *minor.*

Exercise 3: Synonyms

Scan the readings to find the words on the left. Carefully read the sentences in which the words appear. Then match each word with its synonym or definition.

1. infrastructure	a. next
2. structure	b. beliefs
3. distortion	c. twisting, bending out of shape
4. assistance	d. gas, water, electricity
5. utilities	e. foundation
6. philosophy	f. examining
7. inspecting	g. building
8. adjacent	h. aid
9. prospects	i. possibilities

Exercise 4: Antonyms

Match the target vocabulary words on the left with their opposites. The vocabulary items may not use the same meaning used in the readings. Use a dictionary if necessary.

1. achieve	a. past
2. generation	b. fail
3. prospective	c. destruction
4. contrary	d. discard
5. utilize	e. similar

The Grammar of Words and Word Families

Another useful strategy for learning a word is to pay attention to its grammar. What word family does it belong to? If the word is a verb, is it regular or irregular? If it is a noun, is it countable or not countable? If it is an adjective, is it generally followed by a preposition? Part of what is involved in learning a word is paying attention to the grammatical patterns in which the word occurs.

Words can be learned as **derivatives,** as parts of word families. Consider the word *criticize.*

Noun (n.)	*criticism*
Noun (person) (n.)	*critic*
Verb (v.)	*criticize*
Adjective (adj.)	*critical*
Adverb (adv.)	*critically*

As you are learning derivatives, remember that not all words have every part of speech in their word family.

Exercise 5: Word Families

Use these words to fill in the word family chart. Follow the example given. Some words may be used more than once.

<u>achieve</u> achievable achievement achiever	<u>adjacent</u>	<u>assist</u> assistance assistant assisted	<u>contrary (3x)</u> contrarian contrarily contrariness
<u>distort</u> distorted distortion	<u>foundation</u> foundational	<u>generation</u> generate generational	<u>infrastructure</u> infrastructural
<u>innovate</u> innovation innovative innovatively innovator	<u>inspect</u> inspection inspector	<u>nevertheless</u>	<u>philosophy</u> philosopher philosophical philosophize
<u>prospect (2x)</u> prospective prospectively prospector	<u>structure (2x)</u> structural structuralism structuralist structured	<u>utilize</u> utility utilizable utilization	

Noun	Noun (person)	Verb	Adjective	Adverb
achievement	achiever	achieve	—	achievable
—	—	—	—	adjacent
		assist		—
		—	—	contrary
	—		distorted	—
foundation	—	—		—
generation	—			—
infrastructure	—	—		—
		innovate		
		inspect	—	—
—	—	—	—	nevertheless
philosophy				—
prospect				
structure				—
	—	utilize		—

Exercise 6: Word Forms

Complete each sentence with the correct form of the word in parentheses. Add prefixes and suffixes as necessary, and follow spelling rules.

1. (assist) While they were working on the project, ______________ were paid $150 per day and had the use of a company car.

2. (innovate) How did you think of such an ______________ idea?

3. (contrary) I don't dislike modern architecture. On the ______________, I love the geometric houses designed by modernists like Neutra and Schindler.

4. (philosophy) As a college student, I used to sit around in cafes and ______________ with my friends until the early hours of the morning.

5. (prospect) Marianna wants to get married. To save time and trouble, she is using Internet dating sites to find ______________ grooms.

6. (utilize) Google was founded by Larry Page and Sergey Brin while they were students at Stanford University. Their service is now ______________ by people all over the world.

Understanding Words in Context

What can you do when you encounter a word you don't know? One strategy is to consult a dictionary. Sometimes, though, you can guess the meaning of a word or phrase by using context clues, if they are available. There are various types of context clues (clues are in italics).

a. a brief definition or synonym

The great weight of the Imperial Hotel caused it to **subside**, or *sink*, continuously on its unstable concrete foundation.

b. an example

Homes built in Wright's **Prairie style of architecture,** including both *Taliesin and Fallingwater,* were characterized by open interior spaces, horizontal lines, and low-pitched roofs.

c. a contrast

Unlike the dark, boxed-in, **cluttered** homes of the Victorian era, homes in the Prairie style were light, open, and *minimally decorated.*

d. an inference

Taliesin was the name of a Welsh *poet,* a Druid-bard who *sang* to Wales the glories of fine art.

e. a definition or direct explanation

In 1936, during the Great Depression, Wright developed *a simplified form of the Prairie style* called "**Usonian**."

Exercise 7: Context Clues

Read the passages. Then identify which of the context clues suggests the meaning of the underlined word or phrase: (a) brief definition or synonym, (b) an example, (c) a contrast, or (d) a direct explanation.

_____ 1. Wright studied Japanese earthquakes and found them to be "a *wave-movement*, not of sea, but of earth. Because of the wave movements, deep foundations like long piles would oscillate and *rock* the structure."

_____ 2. In architecture, a cantilever is *any structural element that extends out and beyond its supporting wall and is thus supported on only one end.*

_____ 3. Some people criticized Fallingwater because of flaws in its design. *Cracks* would appear in the concrete, be repaired, and then reappear; terraces intended to be parallel to the ground were obviously *less than straight.*

_____ 4. The place was to be self-sustaining if not self-sufficient, and with its domain of two hundred acres was to be shelter, food, clothes, and even entertainment within itself.

_____ 5. In 1923, Tokyo and Yokohama were devastated in the greatest earthquake in Japanese history. *Comparatively*, the Imperial Hotel suffered only *minor* damage.

Exercise 8: Word Meanings in Context

Scan Readings 1, 2, and 3 for the words and phrases. The number of the paragraph containing the word or phrase is given in parentheses. Circle the letter of the meaning that best fits the context of the reading passage. Write the words or phrases that served as clues on the lines.

1. eventually (4)
   a. immediately
   b. within 5 or 10 years
   c. after a long time
2. was aware (5)
   a. recognized, understood
   b. worried
   c. didn't believe
3. tremblor (5)
   a. mud
   b. ocean wave
   c. earthquake
4. scanned (10)
   a. walked
   b. looked
   c. bought
5. site (17)
   a. location
   b. young man
   c. waterfall
6. adjacent (20)
   a. beneath
   b. next to
   c. around
7. emphasized (20)
   a. hid
   b. stressed
   c. apologized for

1. ______________________________
2. ______________________________
3. ______________________________
4. ______________________________
5. ______________________________
6. ______________________________
7. ______________________________

Exercise 9: Similar Meanings

The words in the chart are similar in meaning. Study the examples. Notice the differences in sentence structure and punctuation.

nevertheless, however, still	The Kaufmanns and their guests took great pleasure in Fallingwater. **Nevertheless,** the risks were real. Kaufmann himself never felt sure that the building was safe.
although, though, even though	**Although** the Kaufmanns and their guests took great pleasure in Fallingwater, the risks were real.
but, yet	The Kaufmanns and their guests took great pleasure in Fallingwater**, yet** the risks were real.

Fill in the blanks with one of the words or phrases from the chart.

1. The Imperial Hotel was gorgeous, __________________ it was not the engineering marvel that Wright said it was.

2. __________________ the house was beautiful, it had to be torn down and rebuilt because the foundation was cracked.

3. Frank Lloyd Wright designed more than 1,000 structures in his career. __________________, only about 500 of them were built.

4. Wright was most famous for designing homes. __________________, he also designed furniture, windows, and even a gas station in Cloquet, Minnesota.

5. __________________ Wright worked almost constantly during his long career, his family life was not as stable. He was married and divorced several times, and one of his mistresses was murdered at Taliesin.

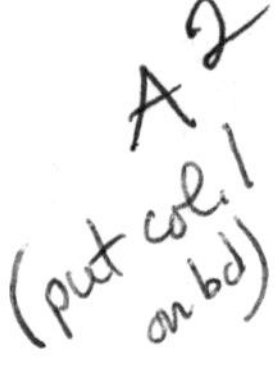

Exercise 10: Verb-Preposition Collocations

Look at the verbs used in the readings. The number in parentheses is the paragraph number. Write the preposition that follows each.

1. adapted __________ (2)
2. used __________ (3)
3. return __________ (5)
4. live __________ (10)
5. arranged __________ (12)

Match these verbs with preposition they commonly collocate with.

6. designed	a. with
7. aware	b. by
8. assist	c. about
9. plan	d. of
10. care	e. to

Verbs are often followed by the same prepositions. Write other verbs you can think of that collocate with the prepositions.

from	for	by	of	to
__________	__________	__________	__________	__________
__________	__________	__________	__________	__________
__________	__________	__________	__________	__________

Using Words in Communication

Exercise 11: Reading and Speaking

The timeline on page 26 includes some of the most important buildings designed by Frank Lloyd Wright during his 70-year career. Select one building, and do research about it. Try to find the answers to the questions. If possible, print a picture of the building. Use the picture and your notes to prepare an oral report on the structure you selected.

1. What is the name of the building?
2. Is it a house or commercial structure?
3. For whom did Wright design the structure? Where is it located?
4. When did construction begin? When was it completed?
5. What is the style of the structure, if any?
6. What does the structure look like? What are its distinguishing features?
7. Is the structure still standing today? Can visitors see it?

Timeline of Frank Lloyd Wright's Career	
1889–1909 **Oak Park period**	1889 Wright home, Oak Park, Illinois 1891 Charnley House, Chicago, Illinois 1894 Winslow House, River Forest, Illinois 1905–1908 Unity Temple, Oak Park, Illinois
1900–1917 **Prairie Houses**	1907 Westcott House, Springfield, Ohio 1909 Robie House, Chicago, Illinois 1911 Taliesin, Spring Green, Wisconsin
1920s **Post-Prairie period**	1929, Graycliff, Buffalo, New York 1934 Fallingwater, Pittsburgh, Pennsylvania
1930s **Usonian period**	1936 S.C. Johnson & Sons Co. Administration Building, Racine, Wisconsin 1936–1937 First Herbert Jacobs House, Madison, Wisconsin 1937 Taliesin West, Scottsdale, Arizona 1939 Sturges House, Brentwood Heights, California
1940s	1943 Guggenheim Museum, New York City (completed 1959) 1944 S. C. Johnson & Sons Co. Research Tower, Racine, Wisconsin
1950s **Usonian Automatic period**	1952 Price Tower, Bartlevsille, Oklahoma 1954 Beth Shalom Synagogue, Elkins Park, Pennsylvania 1955 Toufic Kalil House, Manchester, New Hampshire

Exercise 12: Writing

Write a three-paragraph essay about the structure you selected in Exercise 10. Organize your essay this way:

Paragraph 1: Questions 1–4

Paragraph 2: Questions 5–6

Paragraph 3: Question 7

As much as possible, use the target vocabulary from this unit.

Exercise 13: Critical Thinking

These questions will help you develop your critical-thinking skills. Critical thinking helps you evaluate information and reach logical conclusions using the information that is given. Ask yourself the questions as you work on your answers: What information in the reading supports my answer? What other information do I have that supports my point of view? Where can I get more information about the topic?

1. Look at the photos of the three structures discussed in the readings, and reread the descriptions in the readings. How are the structures similar? How are they different? Consider these points:
   - philosophy or concept
   - design
   - building materials
   - site and setting
2. Which Wright structure—house or building—do you like the best? Why?
3. If you were going to design your own house, which features of Wright's style would you like to include, if any?
4. In your opinion, what was Frank Lloyd Wright's greatest achievement? How will future generations remember him?

Hunt
fraud
revealed
Webster
Louis
another
Hoover
death
Nixon
Robert
Justice
one
extortion
variety
President
halt
highly
convicted
U.S
originally
inquiry
controversial
subversive
files
director
FBI
kidnapping
property
role
Kelley
era
Academy
public
division
conspirators
investigations
Investigation
powers
designated
yielded
William
actually
belonging
reorganized
conducted
acting
Hoover's
Bureau
years
raising
final
Freehand
Congress
civil-rights
served
Richard
gradually
White
local
added
Clarence
crime
except
Created
Edgar
stolen
among
affair
charged
assigned
espionage
wide
Sessions
Patrick
battle
target
House
Howard
dramatic
activities
Mueller
agency
groups
standards
cover-up
units
attack
cooperated
gambling
attempting
resigned
undertook
wider
organized
Federal
direction
investigative
prohibition
pressure
transportation
police
Dept
interstate
duty
jurisdiction
frequent
break-in
important
Watergate
played
top
matters
government
robbery
officials
became
subsequently
violations
sabotage
destroyed
investigating
Gray
behalf
followed
named
liberal
bank
laws

2

Watergate

Vocabulary Preview

Preview 1

These sentences contain information from the readings. Fill in the blanks with the word that best completes each sentence.

analyzing **evaluate** **investigation** **methodical** **role**

1. The Senate Watergate Committee was responsible for __________________ the presidential tape recordings.

2. Woodward and Bernstein revealed information on John Mitchell's __________________ in gathering information against Democrats.

3. Because of the number of people involved in the Watergate activities, a thorough, __________________ review of the information was necessary.

4. The committee decided to conduct a formal __________________ to determine his involvement in the illegal activities.

5. Journalists need to __________________ the accuracy of their sources to ensure they have factual information.

Preview 2

Look at the way the underlined words are used in the sentences. Match each word with its meaning or definition.

1. Evidence about other illegal activities also appeared that pointed guilt to people higher up in the <u>hierarchy</u>.
2. One question that still remains is why did Nixon and people in the government <u>undertake</u> illegal activities and think that they wouldn't get caught?
3. Woodward and Bernstein <u>acknowledge</u> that their story could not have been written without the information provided by Deep Throat.
4. For his graduate school thesis, Fred Weisberger established five <u>criteria</u> to evaluate 120 possible Deep Throat suspects.
5. One <u>outcome</u> of the Watergate scandal and the *Post's* involvement was that national media do help shape events.

_____ 1. **hierarchy**	a. to accept or admit that something is true
_____ 2. **undertake**	b. standards by which something is judged or decided upon
_____ 3. **acknowledge**	c. the result of an activity or process
_____ 4. **criteria**	d. to start something
_____ 5. **outcome**	e. a system that arranges people or things based on level of importance or status

Reading Preview: What Do You Already Know?

Circle the correct answer. If you don't know the answer, guess.

1. The Watergate scandal happened during the early
   a. 1950s
   b. 1960s
   c. 1970s
   d. 1980s
2. Woodward and Bernstein worked for
   a. *The New York Times*
   b. *The Washington Post*
   c. *The Chicago Tribune*
   d. *The Los Angeles Times*
3. Katharine Graham's Pulitzer Prize–winning autobiography was titled
   a. *The Secret Man*
   b. *All the President's Men*
   c. *Personal History*
   d. *The Final Days*
4. Deep Throat worked for
   a. the FBI
   b. the Supreme Court
   c. the Republican party
   d. the U.S. Defense Department
5. The Watergate scandal led to
   a. Nixon's resignation
   b. a new interest in journalism
   c. a review of the role of media and the government
   d. all of the above

Review this timeline before you read the readings, but refer to it as necessary as you complete this unit.

Washington Post *Timeline of Watergate Events*	
June 1972	Five men are arrested as they are trying to break into the Democratic National Committee Headquarters at the Watergate apartment complex in Washington, DC.
August 1972	A check for $25,000, contributed to the Nixon campaign, ends up in the bank account of one of the burglars. When asked about the check, John Mitchell, who had been attorney general and was now head of the Nixon re-election campaign, denies any **administration** link to the check or the burglary.
September 1972	The *Post* reveals that Mitchell, while serving as attorney general, controlled a secret Republican fund that he used to finance intelligence-gathering operations against the Democrats.
October 1972	FBI agents establish that the Watergate break-in is part of a huge campaign of spying and sabotage conducted by high-level Republicans in an effort to get Nixon re-elected.
November 1972	Nixon is re-elected in a national landslide.
January 1973	Two Nixon aides, G. Gordon Liddy and James McCord, are convicted of conspiracy, burglary, and wiretapping in the Watergate incident.
April 1973	The highest-ranking members of Nixon's staff, H. R. Haldeman, his chief of staff, and John Ehrlichman, his domestic advisor, as well as Attorney General Richard Kleindienst, resign as a result of the scandal. White House counsel John Dean is fired.
May 1973	The Senate Watergate Committee begins to hold nationally televised hearings.
June 1973	In the Senate hearings, John Dean reveals to the committee that he has discussed the Watergate situation with the President at least 35 times. Alexander Butterfield, the president's former appointment secretary, reveals at the hearings that, since 1971, Nixon has recorded all telephone calls and conversations that took place in his office. The Senate Watergate Committee subpoenas* the presidential tapes. Nixon refuses to give the tapes to the Senate Watergate Committee.

***subpoenas** (in law): requests that material or a person be delivered to court

October 1973	The "Saturday Night Massacre": Nixon fires Special Prosecutor Archibald Cox and abolishes the office of special prosecutor. The President's newly appointed attorney general, Elliott Lee Richardson, and the deputy attorney general, William Ruckleshaus, resign when they are asked to fire the special prosecutor. Pressure to impeach* the President grows in Congress.
December 1973	The White House attorneys **acknowledge** an 18½-minute gap in one of the subpoenaed tapes. Judge Sirica* tells the public about the gap.
April 1974	The House Judiciary Committee subpoenas the tapes. The White House releases 1,254 pages of edited transcripts of the Nixon tapes to the Committee, but the Committee insists that the tapes themselves must be given to the Committee.
May 1974	Nixon begins listening to the tapes again and again refuses to give them up.
July 1974	The U.S. Supreme Court unanimously rejects the President's claim of executive privilege and orders him to provide the 64 tapes of recordings of White House conversations. Four articles of impeachment* pass in the House of Representatives.
August 1974	Richard Nixon becomes the first U.S. President to resign. Vice President Gerald Ford becomes President and soon after pardons* Nixon of all charges related to Watergate.

***impeach:** to accuse a public official of misconduct

***Judge Sirica:** chief judge of the U.S. District Court of the District of Columbia

***articles of impeachment:** the set of charges drafted against a public official to remove him or her from office

***pardons:** issues a public announcement of forgiveness

 Introduction to the Readings

(1) Watergate was a politcal scandal in the United States during the 1970s that caused the resignation of a U.S. President (a first), jeopardized the integrity of the U.S. Constitution (because of how the President viewed his power), and led to distrust of the government by the American people. The scandal got its name because it was at the Watergate Office Complex where five men were caught breaking into the Democratic National Committee headquarters. It's worth noting that since Watergate, any political or celebrity-related scandal is often labeled with the word *gate* at the end (for example, *Iran contra-gate, Monica-gate*).

(2) By being the first newspaper to publish the story of *The Pentagon Papers,* the U.S. Defense Department's secret history of the Vietnam War, and the Watergate story that ended the presidency of Richard M. Nixon,* The family-owned *Washington Post* went from a hometown newspaper to a publication of huge national and international consequence and prestige. Suddenly it rivaled the *New York Times.* After her husband's death in 1963, Katherine Graham became president of *The Post* and a legend in U.S. American journalism and business. In 1995, she was named one of the 100 most powerful women in the world.

***Richard M. Nixon:** the 37th President of the United States, 1969–1974. Nixon was a Republican.

(3) Three readings are excerpts from Graham's account of the Watergate scandal* as recorded in her Pulitzer Prize–winning autobiography, *Personal History.* Reading 1 is Graham's description of Bob Woodward and Carl Bernstein, the two reporters mainly responsible for **investigating** and writing about Watergate. Readings 2 and 3 are about her efforts to ensure that her paper would not be sued for libel* and that everything being published in the *Post* was 100 percent true.

***scandal:** bad behavior and public reaction to it

***libel:** (in law) when a statement or picture is published that damages a person's name or reputation

(4) Reading 4 comes from Bob Woodward's book *The Secret Man,* which was written after the **identity** of Deep Throat, Woodward's high-ranking source on the stories about Watergate, was revealed. The reading

describes some of the attempts made to uncover the **identity** of Deep Throat. For many years, people regarded this as one of the best-kept secrets in U.S. American history and a testament to the journalistic ethic of protecting sources. Woodward had originally vowed to protect this source until the death of Deep Throat, but circumstances arose in 2005 that made that impossible. Deep Throat (Mark Felt) died in the spring of 2009.

Reading 1: Bob Woodward and Carl Bernstein—Key Reporters on the Story

Excerpt adapted from *Personal History* by Katharine Graham (New York: Knopf, 1997) pp. 401–2.

(5) Woodward had come to the *Post* fresh from the Navy. Having been accepted by Harvard Law School, he had chosen instead to pursue journalism as a career. He so much wanted to work for the *Post* that the managing editor had instructed his deputy to hire Woodward for two weeks—without pay—and to look at his copy every night to see what he could do. Not one of 17 stories that Bob wrote during those two weeks was ever printed and, at the end of the trial period, the deputy confidently declared that Woodward was a bright and good guy but lacked the skills needed for being a newspaper man—in short, he was hopeless, and would be too much trouble to train. The deputy told Woodward to get some experience and come back in a year. So Bob went off and got a job in a nearby newspaper and, after several months, he began to call the *Post* editor until the editor finally decided to hire him. From that point on, Bob distinguished himself at the *Post*.

(6) Carl Bernstein, on the other hand, had been at the *Post* since the fall of 1966 but had not distinguished himself. He was a good writer but his poor work habits were well known. In fact, one thing that stood in the way of Carl's being put on the story was that Ben was about to fire him. Carl was known for an irresponsible expense account and numerous other delinquencies—including having rented a car and **abandoned** it in a parking lot and then presenting the company with an enormous bill.

(7) But Carl, looking over Bob's shoulder while he reworked parts of the text [of the Watergate stories] immediately got hooked on this strange story and was off and running. Top editors were told that Carl was pursuing the Watergate story with verve,* working hard, and contributing a great deal. It was Carl early on, in fact, who made the first connection of the crisp $100 bills in the pockets of the burglars to the money raised for the Nixon campaign. Managing Editor Ben Bradlee decided to keep him on the story.

*__verve:__ enthusiasm or energy

(8) Woodward and Bernstein clearly were the key reporters on the story—so much so that we began to refer to them collectively as "Woodstein." In September of 1972, their first report on what was to become "The Watergate Scandal" was published in the *Post*. Two weeks later, a seminal* article, also written by them appeared on front page of the *Post*. They had dug up information that there was a secret fund, controlled by John Mitchell and four other people, which was to be used to gather intelligence on the Democrats. Thus the story reached a new level, involving Mitchell himself, not only in his new **role** in the campaign, but when he was still attorney general, since Woodward and Bernstein had unearthed Mitchell-authorized expenditures for the fund from the previous year.

*__seminal:__ important for the future

Reading 2: *The Washington Post*—Its Role in the Watergate Scandal

Excerpt adapted from *Personal History* by Katharine Graham (New York: Knopf, 1997) pp. 460–62.

(9) By October of 1972, five months into the scandal, I was feeling stressed. The constant attacks on us by the Committee to Re-elect the President and by people throughout the Nixon **administration** were effective. During these months, the pressures on the *Post* to stop writing about Watergate were intense and uncomfortable, to say the least. But, unbelievable as the revela-

Carl Bernstein (played by Dustin Hoffman) and Bob Woodward (played by Robert Redford) work on their stories for the Post. *The movie* All the President's Men *was released in 1976 and won four Oscars.*

tions coming out of our **investigations** were, the strong evidence of their accuracy is part of what kept us going.

(10) Many of my friends were puzzled about our reporting. Readers also were writing to me, accusing the *Post* of ulterior **motives,** bad journalism, and a lack of patriotism. It was a particularly lonely moment for us at the newspaper. Other organizations were beginning to report the story, but we were so far ahead that they could not catch up; Woodward and Bernstein had most of the sources to themselves. The wire services sent out our stories, but most papers either didn't run them or buried them somewhere toward the back pages of the newspaper. I sometimes privately thought: If this is such a great story, then why isn't anyone else writing about it?

(11) Bearing the full weight of presidential and public disapproval is always disturbing. Sometimes I wondered if we could survive four more years

of this kind of strain, of the pressures of living with an **administration** determined to harm us. I couldn't help thinking about what condition we'd all be in—including the newspaper—at the end of it. The best we could do under such an attack, I felt, was to keep **investigating,** to look everywhere for hard evidence, to get the details right, and to report accurately what we found.

Reading 3: Watergate and New Journalism

Excerpt adapted from *Personal History* by Katharine Graham
(New York: Knopf, 1997) pp. 506–8.

(12) Watergate was a transforming event in the life of the *Washington Post*—as it was for many of us at the newspaper and throughout journalism. Anything as big as Watergate changes you, and I believe it changed not only the *Post* and me but journalism as a whole. There were both positive and negative effects.

(13) In terms of positive effects, Watergate tested, for all of us at the *Post*, our whole organization: our talents, our skills, our ability to organize and mobilize resources to handle a long-term major **investigation** while still covering the daily news. In addition, ultimately Watergate showed what could be done by reporters relentlessly pursuing **investigative** work, by editors remaining as skeptical,* demanding, and dispassionate as possible under the circumstances, and by editorial writers helping to keep the questions foremost in the minds of our readers.

***skeptical:** doubtful or uncertain

(14) More important in terms of its effects, Watergate propelled the *Post* to true national and international prominence. The newspaper became known throughout the world because of it. On one level, the changed image of the *Post* was flattering; on another, it was both disturbing and distracting to getting on with other things. The positive press we began to get was heady and head-turning stuff, but the world, fortunately, has a way of keeping one humble. If the world didn't do it, I was determined to remind all of us of the need to keep arrogance under control.

(15) Watergate also changed the way journalism and journalists are viewed, and in fact they way they work. During the Watergate affair, we—at the *Post* at least—had developed certain habits that were hard to break. John Anderson, an editorial writer, insightfully discussed this in some notes he made on the editorial page at the time:

> "We had become used to a high degree of tension and drama. Morning editorial conferences were becoming almost frightful, as we went back and forth for hours over each day's events. Quickly they came to take up the entire morning, as we sat around with the papers spread out before us. The *Post*'s triumph in Watergate is well known, but we paid a large price for it which has had little attention. When it finally ended with Nixon's resignation, life for all of us was suddenly less interesting. For a long time afterwards news coverage was uneven and erratic because half the staff, particularly young reporters, were off chasing mini-scandals. It was a matter of years before we got back to consistent, orderly coverage of everyday news such as school boards and county council meetings."

(16) Young people flocked into journalism, some for good reasons and some hoping to be Woodward and Bernstein. Certainly, Watergate provided a great deal of evidence that the national media do indeed shape events. Clearly, press reports contributed to Judge John Sirica's doubts about what he was hearing in his courtroom, to congressional questions, and to public concern. But we didn't set out to have such a major impact. No one—least of all the press itself—thinks we are free from errors and faults or completely without bias. I never once have believed that we in the press do everything right, but we try to keep our opinions to the editorial page.

(17) Also, the normal relationship between the press and the president, usually one of respectfully distant skepticism, was totally destroyed in the case

of Watergate, and that, too, affected journalism. I was somewhat alarmed by certain tendencies toward over-involvement, which I felt we should overcome as quickly as we could. The press after Watergate had to guard against the romantic tendency to picture itself in the **role** of heroic champion of the people, defending all virtues against tyranny of the powerful. Watergate has been a deviation from the normal, and I felt we couldn't look everywhere for conspiracies and cover-ups. On the other hand, I don't believe we "over-covered" Watergate, as some Nixon supporters claimed.

(18) As outstanding as Watergate was to the country and the government, it underscored the **role** of a free, able, and energetic press. We saw how much power the government has to reveal what it wants when it wants to give people only the authorized version of events. We re-learned the lessons of the importance of the right of a newspaper to keep its sources confidential.

(19) The credibility of the press stood the test of time against the credibility of those who spent so much time self-righteously denying their own wrong-doing and assaulting us by questioning our performance and our **motives.** In a speech I made in 1970—before Watergate—I said: "The cheap solutions being sought by the **administration** will, in the long run, turn out to be very costly." Indeed, they did.

Reading 4: Who Was Deep Throat?

Excerpt from *The Secret Man: The Story of Watergate's Deep Throat* by Bob Woodward (New York: Simon & Shuster, 2005) pp. 151–56; 217–19.

(20) Over the years many people have asked me if the **identity** of Deep Throat would ever be disclosed. I don't remember exactly why or when but sometime back in the 1970s I answered that I thought it should be revealed only after his death, unless in his lifetime he changed his mind and agreed to have it disclosed, an unlikely occurrence I believed.

(21) I thought it should be revealed to set the historical record straight. History should know that a critical source was No. 2 in the FBI [Federal

Bureau of Investigation]. Carl Bernstein and Ben Bradlee seemed to agree, though I don't recall having a serious discussion about this decision with either of them. In many ways, it is a policy question that the *Post* could have addressed. So for decades I said his **identity** would be revealed after his death. I regularly made the point, only half jokingly, to large audiences I was speaking to, that if you don't know his **identity,** it was not obvious, but if you did, as I did, it was obvious.

(22) Only two people I knew of questioned this decision. One was the late Lloyd Cutler, the Washington attorney who had been White House counsel to both Presidents [Jimmy] Carter and [Bill] Clinton. Cutler, who died in 2005 at age 87, objected that I had publicly **identified** the late Supreme Court Justice Potter Steward as a key source for the 1979 book I co-authored on the Supreme Court, *The Brethren*. Cutler maintained that other journalists whom he did not **identify** believed that a confidential source [should be kept secret] forever.

(23) The other objection came from former Nixon lawyer Len Garment. In 2003, after Carl and I sold our Watergate papers to the University of Texas, ensuring the **identities** of the sources that were still living would be protected, Garment wrote a [opinion-editorial] piece in *The Wall Street Journal* with the headline "Deep Betrayal." In it he wrote "it is no secret" that he was a source for *The Final Days*, the second Watergate book that Carl and I wrote. Garment said things in confidence "that I do not believe and did not believe even then." He never gave postmortem release, he noted, but realized that history has an interest. He suggested waiting a decent interval of say 20 years after a source's death.

(24) Since then I have encountered no situation in which a confidential source—and I have had dozens of important ones in the **administration** of President George W. Bush—has raised the possibility of extending the confidentiality beyond death.

(25) I could see the allure some found in trying to establish Deep Throat's **identity.** It was a mystery that would not go away. Once it was established, it would also mean that dozens if not hundreds of people once suspects or on

A political Cartoon of President Nixon in a web of tape (a reference to the tapes he wouldn't turn over).

lists, had not been the source. Washington is a city that thrives on secrets but simultaneously abhors them, especially someone else's secrets.

(26) One night I ran into Pierre Salinger, who had been press secretary to President Kennedy. We began talking about secret sources. He said that he had never been able to discover the sources for three of the most important, sensational stories of the Kennedy years. The chief suspect for two of the leaks, he said, was President Kennedy himself, but we would never know for sure.

(27) In 1982, eight years after the publication of *All the President's Men*, John Dean claimed in his book *Lost Honor* that he thought Deep Throat was Alexander Haig, who had been Kissinger's deputy national security advisor during our Watergate stories. Dean later **acknowledged** that he was wrong. Others made periodic efforts.

(28) James Mann, a former *Post* colleague and someone who helped me obtain the job at the *Post* in 1971, wrote an article for *The Atlantic Monthly* in

May 1992 titled "Deep Throat: An **Institutional Analysis.**" He concluded correctly that Deep Throat had to be someone from the FBI, such as Mark Felt or another official there, because the FBI was trying to keep the White House from politicizing or limiting the Bureau's Watergate **investigation.**

(29) Mann claimed that during the summer and early fall of 1972, I repeatedly spoke to him or within earshot of "my source at the FBI" or "my friends at the FBI."

(30) I seriously doubt that I said this, and I hope I was more careful. I believe I was. After the article appeared, I called Mann, an astute* and experienced journalist, then at *The Los Angeles Times*, to complain. I didn't want to sound too high-church about it, but I argued that a confidential source discussion within the newsroom should be protected, and in any case it was not for him to decide to reveal alleged details about my source.

***astute:** showing sound judgment

(31) In addition, I said that I was certain I did not want to talk about an FBI source in any form. Even in discussions with Carl, I referred only circumspectly to "my friend." Why would I be more forthright to Mann or in his hearing? Yet he had reason to say what he did; after all he was right. Mann held his ground but seemed surprised that I was worried 20 years after the fact. After all, he asked, what was there to protect now? I could hardly explain that the relationship between Deep Throat and me had, how should I say, been sour or bumpy. How could I say I felt emotions ranging from unease to something resembling regret? Mann and I had been friends for more than 20 years, one of those relationships that includes lunch every other year or so. The conversation ended icily, and I don't believe there have been any lunches after that.

(32) One of the best **investigative** efforts to determine Deep Throat's **identity** was **undertaken** by Fred Weisberger of Turlock, California, for a master's thesis. He sent me a copy of his 109-page paper filled with lists, maps, and pictures of my old apartment building. Weisberger has systematically considered 120 possible Deep Throat suspects, including Nixon's nephew, Nixon's

brother, and Nixon's personal secretary (Rose Mary Woods). There were names on the list that I didn't even recognize—Daniel Davidson and Viron Vaky, supposedly of the National Security Council staff.

Weisberger **evaluated** each on five **criteria:**

1. A shared past with Woodward.
2. Access to the information.
3. Ability to meet with Woodward.
4. Personal/professional **motive.**
5. Similarities to Deep Throat.

(33) Weisberger concluded that Deep Throat was probably the National Security Council staffers Laurence Lynn or Winston Lord. He wrote a strong disclaimer, saying his **method** was speculative and circumstantial. He also apologized to Lynn and Lord if he was wrong.

(34) Felt made his list of the top 120 suspects, but Weisberger incorrectly said that Felt met only one of the five **criteria:** ability to meet with Woodward. Nonetheless, it was a fine effort that made some thoughtful textual **analysis** of my books and other documents . . . .

(35) Again and again I retraced my steps, the notes, the books, testimony, an occasional lunch with old Watergate players and, most important, I sifted decades of memory. Felt was now shielded from my effort at interrogation, and his own self-interrogation. There were many questions that we would never get to. Highly trained and focused, Felt was a product of the FBI pyramid—the **hierarchy** and the Hoover rules. The climax for Mark Felt was the year 1972—

Mark Felt

Vietnam, the perceived domestic threat, law and order challenged, the presidential election and all its intensity, the Wallace shooting,* the death of Hoover,* the unexpected directorship of Pat Gray, Watergate, thwarted* ambition, and the insistence of a young reporter.

***Wallace shooting:** 1972 assassination attempt on the governor of Alabama, George Wallace

***the death of Hoover:** the death of J. Edgar Hoover, who had led the FBI for 37 years (1935–1972)

***thwarted:** blocked

(36) Watergate moved history, and there is certainly a tendency—on my part and of many others—to associate epic **outcome** with an epic **motive.** Perhaps that is an unnecessary stretch. Felt's **motives** certainly were complicated and not fully explainable. But three decades in the FBI had steeped him in one basic principle: The truth will come out. And in that, in Watergate, and in Nixon's demise, there was a sense of raw justice. And that, maybe, is enough.

(37) There is probably no period in history about which we know so much, no presidency that has been on the autopsy table to have every part dissected and rummaged through so entirely. The multiple **investigations,** the endless memoirs and diaries, the memos and notes—no one keeps anything close to an equivalent record now. The testimony and trials, the thousands of hours of secret tape recordings—Nixon talking to everyone, everyone talking to him, Nixon on the phone, Nixon going on and on. Virtually everyone in Nixon's inner circle finally turned on him—testified or wrote a book, telling about his bitterness and anger and his efforts to break the law and to use his presidential power to settle new and old scores with his enemies, real and imagined. There is so much that no one will ever be able to digest it all. But this autopsy seems nearly complete.

(38) But then, of course, there are always unanswered questions. Those questions lead to more questions, with the circularity of the endless inquest, keeping people like me in business. We can and should always poke at the questions of **motivation.** And we will. There is never a final draft of history.

Comprehension Check

Did you understand the readings? Mark these sentences true (T) or false (F).

_____ 1. Bob Woodward and Carl Bernstein were the two main reporters covering the Watergate story for the *Post*.

_____ 2. The Watergate scandal revolved around illegal activities surrounding the appointment of John Mitchell to President Nixon's cabinet.

_____ 3. *The Washington Post* was often criticized by the Democratic Party during the publication of the Watergate articles.

_____ 4. Initially, many *Post* readers wrote to Graham accusing her of unfair journalistic practices.

_____ 5. The first report on Watergate was published in 1975.

_____ 6. For decades, Woodward felt strongly that the *Post* should have revealed Deep Throat's identity.

_____ 7. Nixon's brother and nephew were both considered Deep Throat suspects in one analysis.

_____ 8. One negative effect of Watergate at the *Post* was that, after it was over, young reporters were more interested in making a name for themselves than in covering the everyday news.

_____ 9. As a result of the Watergate scandal, Nixon was impeached by the House of Representatives.

_____ 10. Deep Throat was an FBI official named Mark Felt.

Word Study

Target Words

abandon	**evaluate**	**method**
acknowledge	**hierarchy**	**motive**
administrate (administration)	**identical (identity)**	**outcome**
analyze (analysis)	**institute (institutional)**	**role**
criteria	**investigate**	**undertake**

Word Parts

A useful way to figure out the meaning of a word is to look at the way it is put together. Consider the parts of these words.

	Prefix	Root	Suffix
interaction	inter-	action	
unanswered	un-	answer	-ed
insightful		insight	-ful
analyst		analyze	-ist
journalism		journal	-ism

Inter- (meaning "between") and *un-* (meaning "not") are prefixes that have been added to the beginning of a word to give it a new meaning. The suffixes *-ed* (making the word an adjective), *-ful* (meaning "filled with"), *-ist* (meaning "one who performs"), and *-ism* (meaning "the act or process of") change the grammar or part of speech.

Exercise 1: Prefixes

If you know that the prefix *inter-* means "between," what would you expect these phases to mean?

1. an *interlibrary* loan

   ____

2. an *interactive* video game

   ____

3. an *intercollegiate* sporting event

   ____

4. an *interdepartmental* memo

   ____

5. an *intergalactic* encounter in a science fiction movie

   ____

Exercise 2: Roots

The root *-arch-* means "first, chief, rule." Match each word on the left with its definition on the right by writing the letter of the correct definition on the line.

_____ 1. monarch	a. a man who controls a group (usually a family)
_____ 2. matriarch	b. a king or queen who rules an empire
_____ 3. hierarchy	c. a woman who controls a group (usually a family)
_____ 4. patriarch	d. the main enemy
_____ 5. archenemy	e. a group that controls an organization and is divided into levels

Exercise 3: Suffixes

When the suffixes *-ate* or *-ize* are added to words, verbs are often formed. Look at the way the underlined words are used in the sentences. Then match each word with the correct definition.

1. Every semester, the students evaluate the effectiveness of their instructor.

2. The decision to institutionalize family members with dementia or other mental illnesses is difficult to make.

3. The president authorized all of the senior marketing managers to increase spending on television advertising.

4. The detectives decided to investigate why the millionaire had closed two of her back accounts just two days before her death.

5. In order to motivate her son to finish cleaning his room, she offered to take him to the park in an hour.

_____	1. **evaluate**	a. to give power, permission, or approval to someone
_____	2. **institutionalize**	b. to study the facts about something or someone
_____	3. **authorize**	c. to put someone in a health care facility
_____	4. **investigate**	d. to give someone a reason to do something
_____	5. **motivate**	e. to judge the value or condition of something

Word Relationships

Exercise 4: Synonyms

Four of the words in each series have similar meanings. Cross out the word that has a different meaning.

1. plan	manner	procedure	method	disorder
2. start	forgo	undertake	attempt	take on
3. unlike	matching	same	duplicate	identical
4. aim	motive	obstacle	influence	cause
5. leave	quit	abandon	give up	keep

Exercise 5: Related Words

Although *reporter* and *commentator* are often entered in dictionaries as synonyms, these words do not have the exact same meaning.

> A *reporter* is a person who provides the reader or listener with the news as it is happening. For example, if a tornado hits an area of the country, the reporter will give a basic account of the event: Where did it happen? When? How many people were killed or injured? How much damage has occurred?
>
> A *commentator*, on the other hand, is someone who has the time to reflect on what is happening, to analyze particular events, fit them into other larger events, and relate them to broader issues and trends. After the tornado is over, a commentator might write or talk about the costs of providing federal help for tornado victims, the effect of this year's tornadoes on farm production, or the effectiveness of weather reports in preparing people for tornadoes.

For each journalistic event given, indicate whether it is likely to be covered by a reporter (R) or a commentator (C).

1. _____ an airplane crash
2. _____ possible reasons for the increasing number of airplane crashes over the past year
3. _____ an approaching hurricane
4. _____ an analysis of TV violence on real-life violent acts
5. _____ a raging forest fire

The Grammar of Words and Word Families

Exercise 6: Word Families

Use these words to fill in the word family chart. Some words will be used more than once.

abandon	acknowledge	administrate	analyze	criteria (criterion)
abandoned	acknowledged	administration	analysis	
abandonment	acknowledgment	administrative	analyst	
		administratively	analytic	
		administrator	analytical	
			analytically	
evaluate	hierarchy	identical	institute (2x)	investigate
evaluation	hierarchical	identically	institution	investigation
evaluative	hierarchically	identity	institutional	investigational
evaluator			institutionalize	investigative
			institutionally	investigatively
				investigator
				investigatory
method (2x)	motive (2x)	outcome	role	undertake
methodical	motivate			undertaking
methodically	motivation			
	motivational			
	motivative			
	motivator			

Noun	Noun (person)	Verb	Adjective	Adverb
	—	abandon		—
	—	acknowledge		—
		administrate		
		analyze		
criteria/criterion	—	—	—	—
		evaluate		—
hierarchy	—	—		
	—	—	identical	
		institute		
		investigate		
method	—	—		
motive				—
outcome	—	—	—	—
role	—	—	—	—
	—	undertake	—	—

Exercise 7: Word Forms

Complete each sentence with the correct form of the word in parentheses. Add prefixes and suffixes as necessary, and follow spelling rules.

1. (motive) Many citizens have questioned his ________________ for running for political office at this time.

2. (method) The ________________ review of all the evidence in the murder case eventually led to the discovery of the victim's body.

3. (abandon) The approaching hurricane forced hundreds of people living along the coast to ________________ their homes.

4. (evaluate) The supervisor nervously opened the email message that contained her formal, written performance ________________ from the CEO.

5. (institute) Educational ________________ are usually eligible for discounts on computer equipment.

Understanding Words in Context

Exercise 8: Words in Context

Complete each sentence with one of these words. Change the word form if necessary.

acknowledge administration criteria outcome role undertake

1. Newspapers play a major ________________ in shaping how people view politics and politicians.

2. He has ________________ a thorough search of his biological parents.

3. The majority of the ________________ tasks of the job include filing students' records and sending memos to instructors.

4. She is widely ________________ as an expert in jazz history.

5. One ________________ for admission in the MBA program is work experience.

6. The ________________ of the election will not be determined until the absentee ballots are counted.

Exercise 9: Collocations

Collocations are words that often go together or words that often appear before or after one another. Examples are *federal government* and *school bus*. Write the adjectives next to the nouns with which they commonly collocate.

careful	**final**	**selfish**	**ulterior**
detailed	**government**	**social**	**unexpected**

1. ____________________ analysis
   ____________________ analysis
2. ____________________ outcome
   ____________________ outcome
3. ____________________ hierarchy
   ____________________ hierarchy
4. ____________________ motive
   ____________________ motive

Can you think of other nouns to collocate with each adjective? List them.

1. government ____________________
2. careful ____________________
3. ulterior ____________________
4. final ____________________
5. social ____________________
6. selfish ____________________
7. detailed ____________________
8. unexpected ____________________

Exercise 10: Word Meanings in Context

Read the passages. Then complete the sentences or answer the question by circling the letter of the correct choice.

1. "John Dean claimed in his book *Lost Honor* that he thought Deep Throat was Alexander Haig, who had been Kissinger's deputy national security advisor during our Watergate stories. Dean later acknowledged that he was wrong."

   Later acknowledged means that Dean

   a. defended his beliefs

   b. admitted he was incorrect

   c. changed his mind

2. "They had dug up information that there was a secret fund, controlled by John Mitchell and four other people, which was to be used to gather intelligence on the Democrats. Thus the story reached a new level, involving Mitchell himself, not only in his new role in the campaign, but when he was still attorney general, since Woodward and Bernstein had unearthed Mitchell-authorized expenditures for the fund from the previous year."

   Dug up and *unearthed* are synonyms meaning

   a. finding out the truth

   b. hiding the truth

   c. covering up the truth

3. "As outstanding as Watergate was to the country and the government, it underscored the role of a free, able, and energetic press. We saw how much power the government has to reveal what it wants when it wants to give people only the authorized version of events. We re-learned the lessons of the importance of the right of a newspaper to keep its sources confidential."

   The best title for this paragraph is

   a. The Power of the Government

   b. The Importance of the Freedom of the Press

   c. The Unauthorized Story of Watergate

4. "There is probably no period in history about which we know so much, no presidency that has been on the autopsy table to have every part dissected and rummaged through so entirely. The multiple investigations, the endless memoirs and diaries, the memos and notes—no one keeps anything close to an equivalent record now."

   What does this text say about the Nixon presidency?

   a. not very much is known about it

   b. more investigation is needed

   c. much information has been documented

5. "But then, of course, there are always unanswered questions. Those questions lead to more questions, with the circularity of the endless inquest, keeping people like me in business. We can and should always poke at the questions of motivation. And we will. There is never a final draft of history."

   Circularity of the endless inquest refers to

   a. the constant, ongoing nature of investigative reporting

   b. the confusion that reporters often feel

   c. the repetition of events in history

Using Words in Communication

Exercise 11: Writing

Watch the movie *All the President's Men,* and compare and contrast the portrayals of Bob Woodward and Carl Bernstein in the movie with Graham's and Woodward's descriptions. Also, describe how Deep Throat is portrayed in the movie. Now that you know who he is, what do you think about how he is portrayed in the movie?

Exercise 12: Reading

Review the Watergate timeline on pages 32–33. Pick one of the months on the timeline, and do additional research to find out what else was happening in the United States and world at that time and relate it to Watergate.

Exercise 13: Critical Thinking

These questions will help you develop your critical-thinking skills. Critical thinking helps you evaluate information and reach good conclusions using the information that is given. Ask yourself the questions as you work on your answers: What information in the reading supports my answer? What other information do I have to support my conclusion? Where can I get more information about the topic?

1. What standards did *The Post* practice to make sure that Watergate reports were accurate?
2. What positive effects did covering the Watergate story have on *The Post*?
3. What negative effects did covering the Watergate story have on *The Post*?
4. How do you think newspaper reporting has changed as a result of the Watergate events?

3

Physical Feats

Vocabulary Preview

Preview 1

These sentences contain information from the readings. Fill in the blanks with the word that best completes each sentence.

attain **attribute** **incline** **route** **visible**

1. We can _______________ many of the strange visions and experiences reported by climbers to tiredness and lack of oxygen.
2. To _______________ the goal of reaching the summit of Everest is not to reach the end of the adventure. The climber still has to make the descent, which can be difficult and dangerous.
3. Going down a steep _______________ without rope is especially difficult when the slope is a sheet of ice.
4. A camp just a few hundred feet away might not be _______________ during heavy snow.
5. While experienced climbers may try different paths to the top of Everest, commercial tours will usually take inexperienced climbers along the easiest _______________

Preview 2

Look at the way the underlined words are used in the sentences. Match each word with its meaning or definition.

1. In the untramarathon in Hokkaido, there is a checkpoint at 26 miles. Runners who exceed the time limit when they pass are disqualified from the race.

2. A snack at a rest stop might consist of nutrition packs and maybe some bread or a cookie. And of course, it's important for the runners to have water.

3. At a certain point, a runner might block most of the external world out of her mind. Her focus might narrow to simply her body and to the few yards ahead of her.

4. Most runners do not try to maintain a steady speed throughout a long race. At certain times, their run slows—for some runners, to the point of walking.

5. Tightening of muscles and dehydration are two reasons runners might collapse before reaching the finish line.

_____ 1. **exceed**	a. to continue or to keep
_____ 2. **consist**	b. outside of the body; outside of oneself
_____ 3. **external**	c. to break down or fall down
_____ 4. **maintain**	d. to go over or beyond the limits
_____ 5. **collapse**	e. to be made up or composed of

Reading Preview: What Do You Already Know?

Circle the correct answer. If you don't know the answer, guess.

1. Climber Jon Krakauer's book *Into Thin Air* describes
   a. a dangerous and disastrous climb on Mt. Everest
   b. how helicopters search for missing climbers
   c. why children should experience mountain climbing

2. Lack of oxygen at high altitudes can cause
   a. rocks and snow to slide
   b. climbers experience strange visions and experiences
   c. campfires to extinguish

3. An ultramarathon is
   a. shorter than a traditional marathon
   b. longer than a traditional marathon
   c. the same length as a traditional marathon

4. The length of a marathon is
   a. 10.5 miles
   b. 24.2 miles
   c. 26.2 miles

5. Long distances races have stations where
   a. runners who are tired can be replaced by teammates
   b. runners stop to talk to reporters and sponsors
   c. runners can get food or water or can rest

6. Marathon and ultramarathon runners have to fight
   a. tiredness, pain, and not having enough water in the body
   b. fear, depression, and anger
   c. headaches from the pollution of cars and other vehicles

Introduction to the Readings

(1) Some people like to challenge themselves physically by climbing mountains, running marathons, or competing in triathalons. Why do people choose to do this? What is it about these physical feats that make them so compelling?

(2) Climbing Mount Everest, the world's tallest mountain, is the ambition of many serious mountain climbers. Many excellent climbers have tried to reach the summit of Everest and have succeeded. The extreme high altitude, bitter cold, and severe weather test the physical endurance and skills of everyone who tries to climb it. In the 1960s and 1970s, only the very best and most experienced climbers could attempt to climb Everest. More recently, however, commercial "adventure tours" have made it possible for relatively inexperienced climbers to try to climb this mountain.

(3) Jon Krakauer is an experienced climber who has written several books about climbing mountains and the outdoors. His book *Into Thin Air* documents a commercial Mount Everest expedition during 1996 that turned into a disaster. The two expedition leaders, Rob Hall and Scott Fischer, and six of the climbers died on the mountain. The excerpts describe Krakauer's climb to the summit of Mount Everest and moments during his descent.

(4) Haruki Murakami is a fiction writer whose works have been translated into many languages. In 1982, he sold the bar that he owned to devote a year to his writing and began running to stay in shape. In his book *What I Talk about When I Talk about Running,* he writes about the influence of running on his writing. In this book, he describes his experiences participating in an ultramarathon—62 miles!

Reading 1: Climbing Up and Descending Mt. Everest

Excerpt adapted from *Into Thin Air* by Jon Krakauer
(New York: Random House, 1997) pp. 187–207.

(5) Bottled oxygen does not make the top of Mount Everest feel like sea level. Climbing above the South Summit with my oxygen tank giving me just under two liters of oxygen per minute, I had to stop and take three or four breaths of air after every step. Then I'd take one more step and have to pause for another four deep breaths. This was the fastest pace I could manage. The oxygen systems we were using delivered a mixture of oxygen gas and outside air. One of the benefits of using oxygen was that it made an elevation of 29,000 feet with gas feel like **approximately** 26,000 feet without gas.

(6) Climbing along the summit ridge,* sucking gas into my lungs, I felt a strange sense of calm. The world outside my rubber mask was bright and clear but seemed not quite real. I felt drugged and separated from the **external** world. I had to remind myself over and over that there was 7,000 feet of sky on either side of me, and that I would pay for a single wrong step with my life.

***summit ridge:** long, narrow part of the top of the mountain

(7) Half an hour above the South Summit I arrived at 40 feet of almost vertical rock and ice known as the Hillary Step. . . . It was a slow process, and toward the top I began to wonder whether I might run out of oxygen. Walking slowly up the last few steps to the summit, I felt as if I were underwater and moving at quarter speed. And then I found myself on top of a thin wedge of ice littered with a discarded oxygen cylinder and an old aluminum survey pole,* with nowhere higher to climb. Far below, down a side of the mountain I had never seen, the dry, brown earth of Tibet stretched to the horizon.

***survey pole:** used to walk mountains

(8) Reaching the top of Everest is supposed to cause a feeling of intense happiness; after all, after great difficulties, I had just **attained** a goal I'd had since my childhood. But the summit was really only the halfway point. Any

Mt. Everest is the tallest mountain in the world. It is located in the Himalayan Mountains on the border between Tibet and Depal. It has a height of 29,021 feet or 8,848 meters.

impulse I might have felt to congratulate myself was canceled by my fears of the long, dangerous descent that lay ahead. . . .

(9) Daylight was fading as I descended safely a few hundred feet down a broad gentle snow-filled valley, but then things began to get difficult. The **route** wandered through broken rock that was covered with six inches of new snow. Getting through this confusing, slippery area took complete concentration, which was almost impossible in my exhausted condition. . . .

(10) Some minutes later I had another sensation of not being able to breathe, and I realized my oxygen had once again run out. I pulled the mask from my face, left it hanging around my neck, and kept going, surprisingly unconcerned. However, without the supplemental oxygen, I moved more slowly, and I had to stop and rest more often.

(11) There are many stories about the strange visions and experiences on Everest that are **attributed** to lack of oxygen and fatigue. I gradually became aware that my mind was behaving in a similar fashion, and I observed my own slide from reality with a mixture of fascination and horror. I was so exhausted

that I felt detached from my body, as if I were observing myself from a few feet overhead. I imagined that I was dressed in a green sweater and business shoes. And although the windchill was more than 70 degrees below zero Fahrenheit, I felt strangely warm.

(12) Now there was only one thing between me and the safety of camp: an **incline** of hard glassy ice that I would have to descend without a rope. The tents, no more than 650 horizontal feet away, were only sometimes **visible** through the snow. Worried about making a critical mistake, I sat down to rest and collect my energy before I went any further. Once I sat down I felt no impulse to get up again. It was easier to remain at rest than to cross the dangerous ice slope.

(13) Eventually I stood up and started down the ice, which was as smooth and hard as the surface of a bowling ball. Fifteen difficult, tiring minutes later I was safely at the bottom of the **incline.** I found my pack and in another ten minutes was in the camp itself. I got into my tent with my crampons* still on, zipped the door tight, and lay across the icy floor too tired to sit upright. For the first time I had a sense of how drained I really was: I was more exhausted than I'd ever been in my life. But I was safe. We had climbed Everest.

***crampons:** set of spikes attached to the bottom of climbing boots used for climbing on ice and snow

Reading 2: Running an Ultramarathon

Exceprt from *What I Talk about When I Talk about Running*
by Haruki Murakami (New York: Knopf, 2008), pp. 100–16.

(14) This 62-mile ultramarathon takes place every year at Lake Saroma, in June, in Hokkaido. The rest of Japan is in the rainy season then, but Hokkaido is too far north. Early summer in Hokkaido is a very pleasant time of year, though in its northernmost part, where Lake Saroma is, summer warmth is still a ways off. In the early morning, when the race starts, it's still freezing and you have to wear heavy clothes. As the sun gets higher in the sky, you gradually warm up, the runners . . . shed one layer of clothes after another. By the end of

the race, though I kept my gloves on, I'd stripped down to a tank top, which left me feeling chilly. If it rained, I'd really have frozen, but fortunately, despite the lingering cloud cover, we didn't get a drop of rain.

(15) The **route** takes runners around the shores of Lake Saroma, which faces the Sea of Okhotsk. Only once you actually run the course do you realize how ridiculously huge Lake Saroma is. . . . As courses go—assuming you can afford to take in the view—it's gorgeous. . . . Beside the road cows are lazily chewing grass. They show zero interest in the runners. They're too busy eating grass to care about all these whimsical people and their nonsensical activities. And for their part, the runners don't have the leisure to pay attention to what the cows are up to, either. After 26 miles there's a checkpoint about every six miles, and if you **exceed** the time limit when you pass, you're automatically disqualified. They're very strict about it, and every year a lot of runners are disqualified. After travelling all the way to the northernmost reaches of Japan to run here, I certainly don't want to get disqualified halfway through. No matter what, I'm determined to beat the posted **maximum** times. . . .

(16) I don't have much to say about the first part of the race, to the rest station at the 34th mile. I just ran on and on, silently. It didn't feel much different from a long Sunday-morning run. I calculated that if I could **maintain** a jogging pace of nine and a half minutes per mile, I'd be able to finish in ten hours. Adding time to rest and eat, I expected to finish in less than eleven hours. (Later I found out how overly optimistic I was.)

(17) At 26.2 miles there's a sign that says, "This is the distance of a marathon." There's a white line painted on the concrete indicating the exact spot. I exaggerate only a bit when I say that the moment I straddled that line a slight shiver went through me, for this was the first time I'd ever run more than a marathon.

(18) After I passed that point, and as I was coming up on 31 miles, I felt a slight change physically, as if the muscles of my legs were starting tighten up. I

Marathons (races of 26 miles) are common in the United States (especially those in Boston and New York City) and some other countries.

was hungry and thirsty, too. I'd made a mental note to remember to drink some water at every station, whether or not I felt thirsty, but even so . . . thirst kept pursuing me. I felt slightly uneasy. I'd only finished half the race, and if I felt like this now, would I really be able to complete 62 miles?

(19) At the rest stop at 34 miles I changed into fresh clothes and ate a snack. . . . I changed my ultramarathon shoes (there really are such things in the world) from a size eight to a size eight and a half. My feet had started to swell up, so I needed to wear shoes a half size larger. It was cloudy the whole time, with no sun getting through, so I decided to take off my hat, which I had on to keep the sun off me. I'd worn the hat to keep my head warm, too, in case

it rained, but at this point it didn't look like it was going to. It was neither too hot nor too cold, ideal conditions for long-distance running. I washed down two nutrition-gel packs, took in some water, and ate some bread and butter and a cookie. I carefully did some stretching on the grass and sprayed my calves with a little anti-inflammatory. I washed my face, got rid of the sweat and dirt, and used the restroom.

(20) I must have rested about ten minutes or so, but never sat down once. If I sat down, I felt, I'd never be able to get up and start running again.

(21) "Are you okay?" I was asked.

(22) "I'm okay," I answered simply. That's all I could say.

(23) After drinking water and stretching, I set out on the road again. Now it was just run and run until the finish line. As soon as I set off again, though, I realized something was wrong. My leg muscles had tightened up like a piece of old, hard rubber. I still had lots of stamina,* and my breathing was regular, but my legs had a mind of their own. I had plenty of desire to run, but my legs had their own opinion about this.

***stamina:** the ability to work or exercise for a long time

(24) I gave up on my disobedient legs and started <u>focusing</u> on my upper body. I swung my arms wide as I ran, making my upper body swing, <u>transmitting</u> the momentum to my lower body. Using that momentum, I was able to push my legs forward (after the race, though, my wrists were swollen). Naturally, you can only go at a snail's pace running like this, in a form not much different from a fast walk. But ever so slowly, as if it dawned on them again what their <u>job</u> was, or perhaps as if they'd resigned themselves to fate, my leg muscles began to perform <u>normally</u> and I was able to run pretty much the way I usually run. Thankfully.

(25) Even though my legs were working now, the 13 miles from the 34-mile rest stop to the 47th mile were excruciating. I felt like a piece of beef being run, slowly, through a meat grinder. I had the will to go ahead, but now my whole body was rebelling. It felt like a car trying to go up a slope with the

parking brake on. My body felt like it was falling apart and would soon come completely undone. Out of oil, the bolts coming loose, I was rapidly slowing down as one runner after another passed me. A tiny old woman around age 70 or so passed me and shouted out, "Hang in there!" What was going to happen the rest of the way? There were still 25 miles to go.

(26) As I ran, different parts of my body, one after another, began to hurt. First my right thigh hurt like crazy, then that pain migrated over to my right knee, then to my left thigh, and on and on. All the parts of my body had their chance to take center stage and scream out their complaints. They screamed, complained, yelled in distress, and warned me that they weren't going to take it anymore. For them, running 62 miles was an unknown experience, and each body part had its own excuse. I understood completely, but all I wanted them to do was be quiet and keep on running. I tried to talk each body part into showing a little **cooperation**. . . .

(27) Ultimately, using every trick in the book, I managed to grit my teeth and make it through 13 miles of sheer torment.

(28) *I'm not a human. I'm a piece of machinery. I don't need to feel a thing. Just forge on ahead.*

(29) That's what I told myself. That's about all I thought about, and that's what got me through. If I were a living person of blood and flesh, I would have **collapsed** from the pain. There definitely was a being called me right there. And **accompanying** that is a consciousness that is the self. But at that point, I had to force myself to think that those were convenient forms and nothing more. It's a strange way of thinking and definitely a very strange feeling—consciousness trying to deny consciousness. You have to force yourself into an inorganic place. Instinctively I realized that this was the only way to survive.

(30) *I'm not a human. I'm a piece of machinery. I don't need to feel a thing. Just forge on ahead.*

***mantra:** a word or saying as a form of meditation or prayer

(31) I repeat this like a mantra.* A literal, mechanical repetition. And I try hard to reduce the perceptible world to the narrowest **parameters.** All I can see is the ground three yards ahead, nothing beyond. My whole world **consists** of the ground three yards ahead. No need to think beyond that. The sky and wind, the grass, the cows munching the grass, the spectators, cheers, lake, novels, reality, and the past, memory—these mean nothing to me. Just getting me past the next three yards—this was my tiny reason for living as a human. No, I'm sorry—as a machine.

(32) Every three miles I stop and drink water at a water station. Every time I stop briskly to do some stretching, my muscles are as hard as week-old cafeteria bread. I can't believe these are really my muscles. At one rest stop there are pickled plums, and I eat one. I never knew a pickled plum could taste so good. The salt and sour taste spreads through my mouth and steadily permeates* the rest of my entire body.

***permeates:** spreads through

(33) Instead of forcing myself to run, perhaps it would have been smarter if I'd walked. A lot of other runners were doing just that. Give their legs a rest as they walked. But I didn't walk a single step. I stopped a lot to stretch, but I never walked. I didn't come here to walk. I came to run. That's the reason—the only reason—I flew all the way to the northern tip of Japan. No matter how slow I might run, I wasn't about to walk. That was the rule. Break one of my rules once, and I'm bound to break many more. And if I'd done that, it would have been next to impossible to finish this race.

(34) While I was enduring all this, around the 47th mile I felt like I'd passed through something. That's what it felt like. Passed through is the only way I can express it. Like my body had passed clean through a stone wall. At what exact point I felt like I'd made it through, I can't recall, but suddenly I noticed I was already on the other side. I was convinced I'd made it through. I don't know about the logic or the process or the method involved—I was simply convinced of the reality that I'd passed through.

(35) After that, I didn't have to think anymore. Or, more precisely, there wasn't the need to try to consciously think about not thinking. All I had to do was go with the flow and I'd get there automatically. If I gave myself up to it, some sort of power would naturally push me forward.

(36) Run this long, and of course it's going to be exhausting. But at this point being tired wasn't a big issue. By this time exhaustion was the status quo. My muscles . . . seemed to have given up on complaining. . . . My muscles silently accepted this exhaustion now as a historical inevitability, an ineluctable* outcome of the revolution. I had been transformed into a being on autopilot, whose sole purpose was to rhythmically swing his arms back and forth, move his legs forward one step at a time. I realized all of a sudden that even physical pain had all but vanished. Or maybe it was shoved into some unseen corner.

***ineluctable:** not able to escape or avoid something

(37) In this state, after I'd passed through this unseen barrier, I started passing a lot of other runners. Just after I crossed the checkpoint near 47 miles, which you had to reach in less than eight hours and 45 minutes or be disqualified, many other runners, unlike me, began to slow down, some even giving up running and starting to walk. From that point to the finish line I must have passed about 200. At least I counted up to 200. Only once or twice did somebody else pass me from behind. I could count the number of runners I'd passed, because I didn't have anything else to do. I was in the midst of deep exhaustion that I'd totally accepted, and the reality was that I was still able to continue running, and for me there was nothing more I could ask of the world. . . .

(38) If someone had told me to keep on running, I might well have run beyond 62 miles. It's weird, but at the end I hardly knew who I was or what I was doing. This should have been a very alarming feeling, but it didn't feel that way. By then running had entered the realm of the metaphysical.* First there came the action of running, and **accompanying** it there was this entity known as me. I run; therefore I am.

***metaphysical:** reality beyond what the senses perceive

(39) And this feeling grew particularly strong as I entered the last part of the course. . . . The scenery **visible** along the coast is beautiful, and the scent of the Sea of Okhotsk wafted over me. Evening had come on (we'd started early in the morning), and the air had a special clarity to it. I could also smell the deep grass of the beginning of summer. I saw a few foxes, too, gathered in a field. They looked at us runners curiously. Thick, meaningful clouds, like something out of a 19th-century British landscape painting, covered the sky. There was no wind at all. Many of the other runners around me were just silently trudging toward the finish line. Being among them gave me a quiet sense of happiness. Breathe in, breathe out. My breath didn't seem ragged at all. The air calmly went inside me and then went out. My silent heart expanded and contracted, over and over, at a fixed rate. . . . My lungs faithfully brought fresh oxygen into my body. I could sense all these organs working, and distinguish each and every sound they made. Everything was working just fine. People lining the road cheered us on, saying, "Hang in there! You're almost there!" Like the crystalline air, their shouts went right through me. Their voices passed clean through me to the other side.

(40) I'm me, and at the same time not me. That's what it felt like. A very still, quiet feeling. The mind wasn't so important. The mind just wasn't that big a deal.

(41) Usually when I approach the end of a marathon, all I want to do is get it over with, and finish the race as soon as possible. That's all I can think

of. But as I drew near to the end of this ultramarathon, I wasn't really thinking about this. The end of the race is just a temporary marker without much significance. It's the same with our lives. Just because there's an end doesn't mean existence has meaning. An end point is simply set up as a temporary marker, or perhaps as an indirect metaphor for the fleeting nature of existence. It's very philosophical—not that at this point I'm thinking how philosophical it is, I just vaguely experience this idea, not with words, but as a physical sensation.

(42) Even so, when I reached the finish line, I felt very happy. I'm always happy when I reach the finish line of a long-distance race, but this time it really struck me hard. I pumped my right fist into the air. The time was 4:42 PM. Eleven hours and 42 minutes since the start of the race.

(43) For the first time in half a day I sat down and wiped off my sweat, drank some water, tugged off my shoes, and, as the sun went down, carefully stretched my ankles. At this point a new feeling started to well up in me—nothing as profound as a feeling of pride, but at least a certain sense of completion. A personal feeling of happiness and relief that I had accepted something risky and still had the strength to endure it. In this instance, relief outweighed happiness. It was like a tight knot inside me was gradually loosening, a knot I'd never even realized, until then, was there.

Comprehension Check

Did you understand the readings? Mark these sentences true (T) or false (F).

_____ 1. Jon Krakauer was able to reach the summit of Mt. Everest.

_____ 2. Breathing at very high altitudes is not difficult for climbers who use oxygen tanks.

_____ 3. Krakauer had no fear about the descent down the mountain.

_____ 4. Krakauer ran out of oxygen during his descent.

_____ 5. An ultramarathon is held every year in Hokkaido, Japan.

_____ 6. A lot of runners are disqualified at the 26-mile checkpoint because they are already too slow.

_____ 7. The writer of "Running an Ultramarathon" had already run many ultramarathons.

_____ 8. During the race, the writer changed shoes and clothes at a rest stop.

_____ 9. The writer experienced a lot of pain during the race.

_____ 10. In the last part of the race, the writer was running automatically and without much pain.

Word Study

Target Vocabulary

accompany	**consist**	**maintain**
approximate (approximately)	**cooperate (cooperation)**	**maximize (maximum)**
attain	**exceed**	**parameter**
attribute	**external**	**route**
collapse	**incline**	**visible**

Word Parts

Exercise 1: Prefixes

The prefix *co-* means "with" or "together." *Co-* can be added to some nouns and verbs. Add the prefix *co-* to the words to complete the sentences.

author **exist** **operate** **payment** **pilot** **star** **worker**

1. Some insurance companies pay the entire cost of a physical examination, but many require a small _______________ from the patient.
2. My professor plans to _______________ a book with one of her students.
3. The new cashier worked overtime this week because a _______________ called in sick.
4. Amy Adams had a chance to _______________ with Meryl Streep in the movie "Julie and Julia."
5. The _______________ took over the plane when the captain felt sick.
6. People must learn to _______________ with other creatures on the Earth.
7. It's important for everyone to _______________ when a group climbs a mountain together.

Exercise 2: Suffixes

When the suffix *-al* is used to form an adjective, it adds a meaning of "relating to, pertaining to" or "of." Read the information about the meanings of the bold words. Then complete the sentences on page 79 with the correct adjective ending in *-al*.

1. **Exterior** comes from the Latin word **exter**, meaning "outside" or "around."
2. **Geography** is the study of the earth and its physical characteristics.
3. **Norm** refers to a general level or average. It can also be used to describe a standard or pattern, for example, "Having a separate bedroom for each child has become the norm for middle class American families."
4. The Bill of Rights is the name given to the first 10 amendments to the United States **Constitution**. It protects the most basic rights of the people.
5. A **term** is a fixed or limited period of time.
6. A **vocation** is a regular occupation or profession.
7. The bones of a person or animal make up the **skeleton**. **Skeleton** can also refer to any frame or framework, for example of a building or a ship. It can also refer to an outline of an academic or literary work.
8. Play, hobbies, enjoyable exercise, and other pleasant activities "re-create" a person, or "create a person again" by refreshing or renewing him or her. We refer to these activities as **recreation**.
9. The **origin** of something is its source or root. For example, scientists still have many questions about the origin of the universe.
10. A **skeptic** is a person who questions, doubts, or challenges beliefs that others hold to be true.

1. Many Americans consider gun ownership an important ______________ right.

2. Cancer is not always a ______________ illness, especially if it is found early.

3. The city parks department offers some good ______________ programs for children during their summer vacation.

4. If you fall and hit your head hard, go to the hospital. You could be hurt badly, even if there are no ______________ signs of injury.

5. More and more people seem to believe that there is life on other planets, but I am still ______________.

6. Some students at community colleges go on to get four-year, liberal arts degrees. But many are enrolled in programs that provide ______________ training in two years.

7. There are many reproductions of Van Gogh's Starry Night, but to see the ______________ painting, you have to go to the Museum of Modern Art in New York City.

8. Its hard to imagine what the new library will look like. Even though the plans are available on the city website, they are ______________.

9. Many tourists are attracted to Yellowstone National Park every year because of its amazing ______________ features.

10. It is generally considered to be ______________ for American teenagers to sleep until noon on weekends.

Word Relationships

Exercise 3: Synonyms

Synonyms are words with similar meanings, but often the meanings are not *exactly* the same. Read about the pairs of words in bold. Then choose the best word to complete each sentence. Change the form of the word when necessary.

accompany / escort: To *escort* is to *accompany*, but it often implies protection or formal courtesy, sometimes for pay.

1. The president's family is going to ____________ him on his trip to London.
2. Police cars are going to ______________ the suspected terrorist to court because angry crowds are expected to gather on the street.

collapse / fall: *Collapse* and *fall* are similar. However, *fall* emphasizes a sudden vertical drop, and often a hard and sudden landing. Children can *fall* from open windows, for example. *Collapse* is often used when there is a sense of stress, exhaustion, breaking down, crumbling, etc., or when something caves in on itself.

3. The man was on a ladder, painting his house, when he ______________ and broke his arm.
4. On her third day lost in the desert, without food or water, Amanda ______________.

path / route: *Path* can refer to a trail that has been worn by other people. References to *paths* in the woods or mountains are common. It is also common to talk about spiritual *paths*. A *route* carries more of a sense of a specific plan to get from point to point until reaching a final destination. A *route* is often laid out on a map.

5. I like to search both Google and Yahoo for directions before deciding on the best ______________ when I want to get to a place I haven't been before.
6. I tell my children to stay on clear, well-worn ______________ when hiking in the park.

cooperate / collaborate: *To cooperate* is to get along well with others, to work well with others, or to willingly go along with what others want to do. But *cooperation* doesn't necessarily involve a specific end or outcome. To *collaborate* is to work together to achieve a specific outcome or goal. *Collaboration* includes more of a sense of contribution, especially intellectual or mental contribution, than *cooperation* does.

7. Only one scientist received an award, but in fact three others ___________ with him on the project.
8. When Rachel married a man with two children, it was hard for everyone to live together peacefully, at first. But after a few months, everyone learned to ______________.

The Grammar of Words and Word Families

Exercise 4: Word Families

Use these words to fill in the word family chart. Some words will be used more than once.

<u>accompany</u>	<u>approximate (2x)</u>	<u>attain</u>	<u>attribute</u>
accompaniment	approximately	attainability	attributable
accompanist	approximation	attainable	attribution
accompanying			
<u>collapse (2x)</u>	<u>consist</u>	<u>cooperate</u>	<u>exceed</u>
collapsible/able	consistency	cooperation	exceedingly
collapsibility	consistent	cooperative (2x)	excess (2x)
	consistently	cooperatively	excessive
<u>external</u>	<u>incline (2x)</u>	<u>maintain</u>	<u>maximize</u>
externally	inclination	maintainable	maximum (2x)
		maintainability	maximization
		maintenance	maximizer
<u>parameter</u>	<u>route (2x)</u>	<u>visible</u>	
parametric		visibleness	
parametrical		visibility	
		visibly	

Noun	Noun (person)	Verb	Adjective	Adverb
		accompany	——	——
	——		approximate	
	——	attain		——
	——	attribute		——
	——	collapse		
	——	consist		
	——	cooperate		
	——	exceed		
	——	——	external	
	——	incline	——	——
	——	maintain		——
		maximize		——
parameter	——	——		
route	——		——	——
	——	——	visible	

Exercise 5: Word Forms

Complete each sentence with the correct form of the word in paraentheses. Add prefixes and suffixes as necessary, and follow spelling rules.

1. (attain) The ______________ of a gold medal at the Olympics is a dream that very few can achieve.

2. (visible) The climber was ______________ injured. His lips were almost blue, and his head was bleeding.

3. (accompany) A reporter ______________ the cyclists on their ride across the state every year. However, the reporter rides a motorbike.

4. (maximum) The runner reached his ______________ speed in the final mile of the race.

5. (operate) Winning the Iditarod requires great skill on the part of the person handling the dog team, but it also requires the ______________ of the dogs.

6. (consistent) The advisor encouraged him to perform the steps ___________ in order to attain valid results.

Understanding Words in Context

Exercise 6: Words in Context

Complete each sentence with one of these words. Change the word form by adding *-s, -ed, -ing, or -ly* if necessary.

approximate attain attribute consist external maintain parameter

1. Children develop best if parents give them boundaries or limits. Teachers also need to set _______________ for acceptable behavior.

2. At his acceptance speech, the award-winning novelist _______________ his success to the support of his wife and children.

3. Tragically, Bruce Lee died before he _______________ international fame for his role in the movie *Enter the Dragon*.

4. A nuclear family is a family _______________ of parents and their children.

5. Drivers need to _______________ a safe distance between their cars and the cars in front of them in order to avoid rear-end collisions.

6. Insects have _______________ skeletons.

7. _________________ 1,300 people attended the concert.

Exercise 7: Constructing Sentences

Use each set of words to write a sentence. Use all the words given. No additional words will be needed. Add correct capitalization and punctuation.

1. with / freedom / people / it / difficult / is / debt / attain / financial / credit card / for

   ____

2. schools / children / parents / field trips / on / accompany / their / to / invite / elementary

   ____

3. believe / collapsed / historians / understand / believe / is / to / it / civilizations / ancient / why / important

   ____

4. employees / supervisors / prefer / exceed / who / promote / expectations / to

   ____

5. their / reducing / some / maximize / businesses / workforce / by / profits

   ____

6. mountain / of / roads / steep / be / inclines / on / careful

   ____

7. cities / visibility / poor / heavily / in / is / polluted / heavily

   ____

Using Words in Communication

Exercise 8: Reading

Complete the article with the correct word form.

approximate attain attribute collapse maintain route visible

My Triathlon

I live in Chicago, and you could say I'm a serious athlete. Chicago happens to host the world's largest triathlon. So last year, I decided to compete in the main event—the Olympic Distance race. I trained for many months before the race.

The day of the triathlon I got up early. We had to set up our bikes at the transition area by 6:00 AM. I put my shoes, socks, helmet, jersey, and other gear under my bike. I packed a small bag with water and a nutrition bar, and attached it under the seat. I looked around to make sure I could remember the location of my bike easily, and I tied a colorful flag to it to make it more (1) ___________ among the thousands of other bikes. Then I picked up my swimming gear and left for the swim, which starts at Monroe Harbor.

There are too many athletes for everyone to start at once, so participants are organized into "waves" of approximately 150 people. Two minutes before my wave started, we were allowed into the water. I closed my eyes and was able to (2) ___________ a calm, focused state of mind. Then the horn sounded, and I was caught in a frenzy of splashing and thrashing. In that moment, it was hard to (3) ___________ my focus. I panicked. I got off to a slow start. But although I wasn't one of the first people to finish the swim, I wasn't one of the last either. I was already eager to begin the cycling leg as a volunteer reached down to help me out of the water.

I ran the few hundred yards to the transition area and found my bike. I pulled off the flag, put on my socks, shoes, jersey, and finally, my helmet. The bike leg of the course is mostly along a flat (4) ____________—the steepest incline is the ramp leading to Lake Shore Drive, the main road of the course. I'd been cycling long distances daily as part of my training, but I really pushed myself this time, and my legs soon began to cramp. I was breathing hard. I could hardly find the breath to call out to other cyclists as I passed them.

At the finish of the cycling leg, my body wanted to (5) ____________. I wasn't sure what was causing my exhaustion. I (6) ____________ it to lack of sleep the previous night. I'd been up most of the night, too excited to sleep. I thought maybe I'd be unable to finish. But I made it back to transition, where I changed into running shoes and I took off on the last part of the course. And my strength came back. Although I live in Chicago, the city has never been as beautiful to me as it did as I flew along the street from aid station to aid station. I could see the harbor as I ran, and thought about how just a few hours earlier I'd been swimming in it. That thought gave me the extra strength and inspiration I needed as I approached the finish.

I did it. I swam 1.3 kilometers (7) ____________ 9 miles), cycled 40 kilometers (almost 25 miles), and ran about 10 kilometers (a little more than 6 miles). And I didn't come in last.

Exercise 9: Writing

Follow the steps to write three or more paragraphs about a physically challenging event or experience in your own life. As much as possible, use the target vocabulary from this unit.

Step 1: Choose a topic. You can use one of the topics listed, or you can use an idea of your own.

- a sport or athletic event
- a hike or camping experience
- a diet
- an exercise program
- an illness
- a travel experience
- military training
- a physically demanding job
- childbirth

Step 2: Answer the questions on a separate piece of paper.

- What were the difficulties? Were you prepared to face them?
- Was the experience mentally or emotionally challenging, as well as physically challenging? If so, how?
- Were you successful?
- How did you feel at the end of the event or experience?

Step 3: Use your topic in Step 1 and your answers to the questions in Step 2 to write at least three paragraphs about the event or experience.

Exercise 10: Critical Thinking

These questions will help you develop your critical-thinking skills. Critical thinking helps you evaluate information and reach logical conclusions using the information that is given. Ask yourself the questions as you work on your answers: What information in the reading supports my answer? What other information do I have to support my conclusion? Where can I get more information about the topic?

First, answer the questions by yourself. Then share your answers with a partner. Decide on one answer for each question. Be prepared to explain your answers to the class.

1. Why do you think people are attracted to extreme sports or activities such as mountain climbing, running an ultramarathon, or participating in a triathlon? What do you think are some characteristics of people who choose to participate in these types of activities?

2. In recent years, there has been some debate about the responsibilities of government and insurance companies when a person chooses to engage in an activity that involves physical risk. For example, insurance companies have argued that they should not have to pay for injuries suffered by skiers who leave the safety of maintained slopes in favor of remote, difficult inclines. Some people also argue that tax dollars should not be spent on things such as expensive and dangerous helicopter rescues to save people who choose to engage in dangerous activities or who choose to enter areas that are not supervised or maintained. What do you think? If a person chooses to do something dangerous, but not illegal, does anyone have a responsibility to rescue the person in the event of an accident? Who should bear the expense? What about in the case of an illegal activity?

4

To Kill a Mockingbird

Vocabulary Preview

Preview 1

These sentences contain information from the readings. Fill in the blanks with the word that best completes each sentence.

classic **intervenes** **published** **seeks** **summary** **themes**

1. The book *To Kill a Mockingbird* became popular soon after it was _______________.

2. Today the book is considered to be a _______________.

3. The writer uses the voice of a girl to tell a story that explores the _______________ of tolerance and justice.

4. The girl's father, Atticus Finch, is an attorney who _______________ to prove that a black man is innocent of a crime.

5. An opponent in the trial tries to kill the girl and her brother. Boo Radley, the children's strange friend, _______________ and saves them.

6. To give a _______________ of the book, it is necessary to tell the main points of two intersecting stories.

Preview 2

Look at the way the underlined words are used in the sentences. Match each word with its meaning or definition.

1. The author, Nelle Harper Lee, has never wanted fame or attention.

2. Harper Lee didn't grant interviews, except around the time that *To Kill a Mockingbird* became available to readers.

3. Atticus Finch, the attorney in the novel, tries to illustrate the impossibility of the accused man's guilt.

4. Students' essays on *To Kill a Mockingbird* show that the book often leads readers to new insight.

5. In a 1991 survey, the Book-of-the-Month Club found that only the *Bible* ranked higher than *To Kill a Mockingbird* "as making a difference in people's lives."

_____ 1. **author**	a. to give, fulfill, or agree to
_____ 2. **grant**	b. an understanding of the true meaning or the hidden nature of things
_____ 3. **illustrate**	c. the writer of a book, article, poem, etc.
_____ 4. **insight**	d. a sample of data or opinions that can be used to represent what the complete data might show
_____ 5. **survey**	e. to make clear using examples or comparisons, etc.

Reading Preview: What Do You Already Know?

Circle the correct answer. If you don't know the answer, guess.

1. Harper Lee, the writer of *To Kill a Mockingbird,* wrote
   a. many novels
   b. only one novel
   c. a play
2. *To Kill a Mockingbird* is a famous
   a. book about birds that are extinct
   b. painting
   c. best-selling novel and classic movie
3. The plot of *To Kill a Mockingbird* is about
   a. race and injustice before the Civil Rights movement
   b. life and a killing in a small Southern town
   c. a little girl who loves a bird and her brother
4. In the story, an unusual friendship develops between
   a. two children and a strange neighbor
   b. an African-American child and a white child
   c. an attorney and a criminal
5. The father of the children in the story is
   a. an attorney who proves to be greedy
   b. an attorney who proves to be prejudiced
   c. an attorney who proves to be courageous
6. *To Kill a Mockingbird* was
   a. required reading in U.S. high schools for many years
   b. banned by many schools
   c. both a and b

Introduction to the Readings

(1) *To Kill a Mockingbird* was **published** more than 40 years ago, and its American **author** has lived as a virtual recluse ever since, but according to librarians (Museum, Libraries and Archives Council 2004), Harper Lee's *To Kill a Mockingbird* is the one book that everyone should read. It is widely considered the 20th century's most widely read American novel. It has sold more than 30 million copies and, according to many sources, still sells one million copies each year.

(2) The Pulitzer Prize–Winner of 1961 is now considered to be a **classic** novel. It has routinely been at the top of a World Book Day poll **conducted** by the Museum, Libraries and Archives Council (MLA) that asked U.S. librarians which book all adults should read before they die. This novel has been required reading by many U.S. schools for many years. It also did well on another poll about books with favorite happy endings. *To Kill a Mockingbird* explores issues of race and class in the U.S. South in the 1930s through a dramatic court case of an African-American man charged with the rape of white girl.

(3) According to one of the librarians who voted for the book, it "has all the factors of a great read. It is touching and funny but has a serious message about prejudice, fighting for justice, and coming of age." It's a simple story about life in Alabama, but one that has universal appeal. Harper Lee reportedly considered her book to be a love story. More than 40 years later, many regard it as an American masterpiece.

(4) The two readings come from an unauthorized biography of Nelle Harper Lee called *Mockingbird*. The **author,** Charles Shield, tried without success to interview Lee for his book. Lee repeatedly denied requests to **grant** an interview. In the first reading, he explains why he wrote the book and what he hopes readers will learn about Lee and the writing of her novel from his biography. Reading 1 also contains a brief **summary** of the novel.

(5) The fact that Harper Lee never wrote another book and remained out of the public eye for the majority of her life has created speculation and interest in her. According to Shields,

> "I had every intention of writing many novels," [Lee] reportedly said, "but I never could have imagined the success *To Kill a Mockingbird* would enjoy. I became overwhelmed." Every waking hour seemed devoted to the promotion and publicity surrounding the book. Time passed and she retreated from the spotlight, she said. She claimed to be inherently shy and was never comfortable in the limelight. Fame had never meant anything to her, and she was not prepared for what *To Kill a Mockingbird* achieved. Before she knew it, nearly a decade had passed and she was nowhere near finishing a new book. Rather than allow herself to be eternally frustrated, . . . she refused to pressure herself into writing another novel unless the muse* came to her naturally.

***muse:** an inspiration (when lowercased)

(6) In Reading 2, Shields discusses the impact that the book and movie (released in 1962) *To Kill a Mockingbird* had on U.S. society.

Reading 1: Who Is Harper Lee?

Excerpt from *Mockingbird: A Portrait of Harper Lee*
by Charles J. Shields (New York: Henry Holt, 2006), pp. 1–5.

(7) Nelle Harper Lee . . . is the woman who gave the world *To Kill a Mockingbird*, one of the most influential pieces of fiction produced in the United States. In a **"Survey** of Lifetime Reading Habits" **conducted** by the Book-of-the-Month Club in 1991, researchers found that *To Kill a Mockingbird* ranked second only to the *Bible* "as making a difference in people's lives." [More than] 45 years after its **publication,** the novel still draws almost a million readers annually. Maybe that is because its lessons of human dignity and respect for others remain fundamental and universal.

Gregory Peck refers to the best-selling novel on the set of To Kill a Mockingbird.

(8) Despite her novel's huge impact, Lee's writing life has been brief, and her personal life has been intensely private. She wrote only one book, her Pulitzer Prize–winning perennial bestseller, and then, after a brief moment in the spotlight, disappeared from the public eye. She has not **sought** fame, then or since, although around the time of *To Kill a Mockingbird*'s **publication** she did **grant** interviews.

(9) Unlike her lifelong friend Truman Capote (perhaps even because of his example and experience), Harper Lee has never appeared comfortable in the limelight. In fact, not only does she not solicit attention, she also actively discourages it, refusing to speak in public and turning down all requests for interviews and all forms of cooperation with writers and reporters. In our era of relentless and often prurient* self-exposure by some approval-hungry personalities, Lee prefers silence and self-respect. That is not to say she is furtively reclusive; though she enjoys her solitude, she is not some modern-day Emily Dickinson. She lives a normal life, replete with community activities, many related to her church. Lee is "like someone you'd

***prurient:** extreme and unsound; not positive

meet in any small town," as Professor William Smart of Sweet Briar College, in Virginia, expressed it. And Smart has known Lee for [more than] 40 years.

(10) I want readers to be introduced to the **author** and get a sense of what makes her tick: the things that influenced her when she was growing up during the Depression in Monroeville, Alabama, for example; the reasons why classmates regarded her with awe; the traits of non-**conformity** and almost ferocious independence that distinguished her in college; the steps that led to her dropping out of law school and moving to New York to write; the sense of loyalty that drew her to Truman Capote's* side when he was researching his "nonfiction novel," *In Cold Blood*;* the sense of humor that sustained her while she was scrutinized by the media because of the success of *To Kill a Mockingbird* and the film based on it; and finally, the reasons why she never wrote another novel.

Truman Capote/ *In Cold Blood: Truman Capote wrote this groundbreaking book in 1966; it was the first non-fiction novel because Capote as a reporter got so close to the story that he wrote about events and conversations as if he were there.

(11) As I was researching this book, I tended to be asked the same questions by interested friends. The first was, "Is Harper Lee still alive?" Yes. "Nail Har-puh," as her name is pronounced in her hometown, spends most of the year in Monroeville, and a few months in New York in the apartment she has maintained for the [more than] 45 years. Her eldest sister, Alice . . . who is one of the most highly regarded attorneys in Alabama, shares a house with Nelle in Monroeville.

(12) Residents are accustomed to seeing the two ladies puttering around the First United Methodist Church, where they have been members all their lives; at the country club where they enjoy the lunch buffet and the opportunity to see friends; and at various favorite diners around town. Nelle refuses to talk about *To Kill a Mockingbird* in social situations, and friends warn strangers not to bring it up. She has been known to leave the room if pestered about the novel.

(13) The second question I was asked was, "Is she married?" The answer is no. . . . I am not sure what labels Lee would apply to herself, except "woman," "Southerner," and perhaps "writer."

(14) The final question I was continually asked was, "Why didn't she write another novel?" This was the big question I had asked myself in the first place, and which led to the adventure of writing this book. After reading it, I hope you will come away with at least some idea of why she never **published** another novel after *To Kill a Mockingbird*.

❖ ❖ ❖

(15) Years ago, when I was an English teacher in a large high school near Chicago, I taught *To Kill a Mockingbird* to [9th graders]. That's a good time to be introduced to it, because students at that age are crossing the bridge from childhood to young adulthood, as the young characters in Lee's novel are. In-class discussions of the novel tend to be lively, and assigned essays are weighty with **insights** and opinions. It's a very rich text to teach.

(16) If you don't remember much about the novel, here's a **summary:**

(17) *To Kill a Mockingbird* is really two stories. One is a coming-of-age tale told from the point of view of Scout Finch, a girl of about nine, and her slightly older brother, Jem. The second story concerns their father, attorney Atticus Finch, who has been appointed to defend a black man, Tom Robinson, falsely accused of raping a white woman.

(18) There are also two broad **themes:** tolerance and justice. The first is treated through the children's interactions with Arthur "Boo" Radley, their mysterious and maligned neighbor; the second is **illustrated** by Atticus's courageous moral stance in defending Tom Robinson to the best of his ability, despite the racial prejudices of the town. Tying the **themes** together is a homespun piece of advice that Atticus gives Scout: "If you just learn a single trick, Scout, you'll get along a lot better with all kinds of folks. You never really understand a person until you consider things from his point of view. Until you climb inside of his skin and walk around in it." This appeal to recognize the humanity in everyone is practicable in normal day-to-day relations with people, even those we dislike, and, as Atticus powerfully demonstrates, in courtrooms where juries must sit in judgment of their fellow men and women.

Gregory Peck starred as Atticus Finch in the movie version of To Kill a Mockingbird.

(19) The plot of the coming-of-age story revolves around Boo Radley, who is rumored to be a kind of monster living in a shuttered house down the street from the Finches. Scout, Jem, and their next-door neighbor Dill Harris engage in pranks to make Boo show himself. Unexpectedly, however, Boo responds to their interest by reciprocating with small acts of kindness and consideration. They come to feel affectionate about their unseen friend.

(20) The Tom Robinson plot is fairly straightforward. As a black man, Tom doesn't have a ghost of a chance* of being acquitted* of raping a white woman, and Atticus knows he will lose the case. Still, the attorney faces up to the challenge, even stepping between a lynch mob and his client, though racist taunts are directed at Atticus's children.

*__ghost of a chance:__ very small, if any

*__aquitted:__ found innocent

(21) The two plots intersect on a Halloween night not long after the trial is concluded. The drunk father of the girl Tom was accused of having

raped ambushes the Finch children because Atticus exposed his ignorance and vices during the trial. He intends to kill the children, but they are saved by the angelic **intervention** of Boo Radley. Atticus is persuaded by the sheriff not to involve Radley in a homicide case (the children's attacker was killed during the struggle), because it would be cruel, he argues, to subject a pathologically shy man to a sensational trial that would, in any case, end in his acquittal. Atticus is unsure of the moral **implications** until Scout likens the choice to something her father once said: it's a sin to kill a mockingbird "because mockingbirds don't do anything but make music for us to enjoy." Scout escorts Radley back to his home and safety.

Reading 2: *To Kill a Mockingbird* and U.S. American Society

Excerpt from *Mockingbird: A Portrait of Harper Lee* by Charles J. Shields (New York: Henry Holt, 2006), pp. 254–55.

(22) Concern over law and order and civil rights was adding to *To Kill a Mockingbird's* foothold in public schools. Eight percent of public junior high schools and high schools nationally had added the novel to their reading lists only three years after its **publication.** [Lee] marveled at the book's appeal to youngsters: "I find that hard to understand. The novel is about a former generation, and I don't see how this younger generation can like it." . . .

(23) In 1966, the Hanover County School Board in Richmond, Virginia, ordered all copies of *To Kill a Mockingbird* removed from the county's school library shelves. In the board's opinion, the novel was "immoral literature." The episode began when a prominent local physician, W.C. Bosher, the father of a Hanover County student and a county Board of Education trustee, protested that a novel about rape was "improper for our children to read." On the strength of his criticism, the board voted to ban *To Kill a Mockingbird* from the county schools. The next day, the *Richmond News-Leader* editorialized about

the board's "asinine performance." . . . The first fifty students of the local high school who requested a copy of *To Kill a Mockingbird* would receive one gratis, courtesy of the newspaper.

(24) For almost two weeks, the controversy went back and forth on the letters-to-the-editors page, until the *News-Leader* called a halt by allowing [Lee] to have the last word. . . . Eventually, *To Kill a Mockingbird* was restored to Hanover County school libraries because of a technicality in board policy. But the Richmond debate over the book's suitability for young readers was the first of many in the ensuing years. As more schools added *To Kill a Mockingbird* to their reading lists (it reached 74% in 1988), the book also joined the list of the one hundred novels most often **targeted** for banning. . . .

(25) In American culture, *To Kill a Mockingbird* would become like *Catch-22,** *One Flew Over the Cuckoo's Nest,** *Portnoy's Complaint,** *On the Road,** *The Bell Jar,** *Soul on Ice,** and *The Feminist Mystique**—books that seized the imagination of the post–World War II generation—a novel that figured in changing "the system."

**Catch-22:* written by Joseph Heller in 1961, this book satirized World War II and the bureaucracy of war.

**One Flew Over the Cuckoo's Nest:* written by Ken Kesey in 1962, it is considered a study of institutions and their effect on the human mind.

**Portnoy's Complaint:* written by Philip Roth in 1969, it is representative of the coming sexual revolution of the 1960s.

**On the Road:* written by Jack Kerouac in 1951, this is considered the defining book of the "beat" generation.

**The Bell Jar:* written by Sylvia Plath in 1963, it was the first semi-autobiographical book about mental illness.

**Soul on Ice:* written by Eldridge Cleaver in 1968, it established the radical Black writing movement.

**The Feminist Mystique:* written by Betty Friedan in 1964, this book described "the female problem" and led to women's rights movement of the 1960s and 1970s.

Comprehension Check

Did you understand the readings? Mark these sentences true (T) or false (F).

_____ 1. *To Kill a Mockingbird* is told from the point of view of a young girl.

_____ 2. Scout and her brother Jem are the children of an attorney named Atticus Finch.

_____ 3. Boo Radley is an African-American man falsely accused of raping a woman.

_____ 4. Scout and Jem develop positive feelings for Boo Radley because he shows them kindness and consideration.

_____ 5. Atticus Finch defends the children's friend, Boo Radley, in court.

_____ 6. Atticus Finch must face hostility from the town for defending his client.

_____ 7. Racism is an important issue in *To Kill a Mockingbird.*

_____ 8. Many copies of *To Kill a Mockingbird* are still sold every year.

_____ 9. *To Kill a Mockingbird* was made into a film.

_____ 10. Author Nelle Harper Lee died before her book became successful.

_____ 11. Harper Lee wrote *To Kill a Mockingbird* after writing many unsuccessful books.

_____ 12. *To Kill a Mockingbird* was banned in some high schools but taught in many others.

Word Study

Target Vocabulary

author	**illustrate**	**seek**
classic	**implicate (implications)**	**summary**
conduct	**insight**	**survey**
conform (conformity)	**intervene (intervention)**	**target**
grant	**publish (publication)**	**theme**

Word Parts

Exercise 1: Roots

The roots *-duc-*, *-duce-*, and *-duct-* come from the Latin word *ducere*, which means "lead." Look at the way the underlined words are used in the sentences. Then answer the questions on page 104 using complete sentences.

1. Although they may be considered crazy, even by friends and family members, some people insist that they have been abducted by space aliens.
2. Some students study best while listening to music. Others find that listening to music is not conducive to learning.
3. Book clubs sometimes conduct surveys and polls to find out about habits and preferences of readers.
4. There is no such thing as a good orchestra without a good conductor.
5. Companies usually deduct federal and state income tax from employees' paychecks.
6. It is important to educate people about health and nutrition.
7. Meditation can induce very deep relaxation.
8. The government will be taking a greater role in developing a productive workforce.

1. Do you believe in alien abductions?

____

2. For you, what things are conducive to studying?

____

3. Have you ever conducted a science experiment? If so, describe it. If not, what would you like to try?

____

4. What do you think are some characteristics of a good orchestra conductor?

____

5. Do you have a job? If so, is anything deducted from your paycheck? What deductions have you heard about?

____

6. Do you think moral education is primarily the responsibility of parents or of schools?

____

7. How you ever taken a drug or a food product to induce weight loss?

____

8. What do children need to learn to be productive members of society?

____

Exercise 2: Suffixes

The suffix *-ic* means "of," "having," or "pertaining to," and it can be added to some roots and words to form adjectives. For example, the word *idealistic* describes a person who has ideals—an idealist.

A. Match the words with their meanings.

_____ 1. acid	a. a person who writes poems, often as an occupation
_____ 2. altruist	b. a special group or rank
_____ 3. class	c. a solid with six equal square sides
_____ 4. cube	d. a substance (usually in a solution) that has a sour taste and that can react with other substances to form salt
_____ 5. meteor	e. an unselfish person devoted to the good of others
_____ 6. patriot	f. a "shooting star" (a meteoroid lighting the sky as it goes through the earth's atmosphere), or any person who moves or progresses with amazing speed
_____ 7. poet	g. a group of interrelated or interconnected elements that form something larger and more complex
_____ 8. Satan	h. a person who loves, supports, and defends his or her country
_____ 9. system	i. in biblical sources, the chief evil spirit; the enemy of God and humanity

B. Add the suffix *-ic* to the words listed on page 105 to complete the sentences. Follow spelling rules as necessary when adding suffixes.

1. Only novels of the highest quality win awards and continue to rank as bestsellers year after year. *To Kill a Mockingbird* is in this category. It is a _______________ novel.

2. To make health care affordable, it's not enough to ask hospitals and doctors to cut fees. We need to look at insurance and drug industries and at other factors. Our health care problems are _______________.

3. The music is important in writing a good song, but so are the words, or lyrics. In the best songs, the lyrics are _______________.

4. Some people believe that the pentagram and other geometric shapes are _______________ symbols and that they are used in black or evil magic.

5. If you use too much vinegar in a salad dressing, it can taste _____________.

6. Many _______________ young people want to work for peace and social justice.

7. The rental price of some moving trucks depends on how many _______________ feet of space the trucks contain.

8. Even many people who are not especially _______________ believe that military men and women should be appreciated and supported when they return after serving in a war.

9. Sometimes a person who enjoys a _______________ rise to fame will also experience a sudden crash.

Word Relationships

Exercise 3: Synonyms

Three of the words in each series have similar meanings. Cross out the word that has a different meaning.

1. grant	give	take	allow
2. insight	assistance	knowledge	wisdom
3. author	composer	artist	salesperson
4. survey	article	poll	questionnaire
5. theme	idea	topic	criticism
6. target	select	collect	aim
7. illustrate	show	demonstrate	interrupt
8. implicate	connect	value	relate
9. seek	pursue	search	show

Exercise 4: Analogies

Complete each analogy with one of these target words from the unit: *author, conduct, conform, grant, intervene, publish,* or *seek.* The first one has been done for you as an example.

1. **tolerate : agree** is like **yield :** conform
2. **programmer : gamer** is like __________ **: reader**
3. **deny : refuse** is like __________ **: allow**
4. **ignore : permit** is like __________ **: stop**
5. **cook : serve** is like **write :** __________
6. **perform : dance** is like __________ **: poll**
7. **want : have** is like __________ **: find**

The Grammar of Words and Word Families

Exercise 5: Word Families

Use these words to fill in the word family chart. Some words will be used more than once.

<u>author (2x)</u> authorial authorize authorless	<u>classic (2x)</u> classical classically classicalness	<u>conduct (2x)</u> conducive conduciveness	<u>conform</u> conforming conformist conformity
<u>grant (2x)</u> grantable grantedly granter	<u>illustrate</u> illustratable illustration illustrative illustrator	<u>implicate</u> implication implicational	<u>insight</u> insightful
<u>intervene</u> intervening intervention	<u>publish</u> publication publishable publisher	<u>seek</u> seeker	<u>summary (2x)</u> summarily summarize summation
<u>survey (2x)</u> surveyable surveyor	<u>target (3x)</u> targetable targetless	<u>theme (2x)</u> thematic thematically	

Noun	Noun (person)	Verb	Adjective	Adverb
—	author			—
classic	—	—		
	—	conduct		—
		conform		—
		grant		
		illustrate		—
	—	implicate		—
insight	—	—		—
	—	intervene		—
		publish		—
—		seek	—	—
summary	—			
survey				—
target	—			—
theme	—	—		

Exercise 6: Word Forms

Complete each sentence with the correct form of the word in parentheses. Add prefixes and suffixes as necessary, and follow spelling rules.

1. (conform) In many ways, Martin Luther King, Jr., was a ______________.

2. (grant) The Queen of England has been the ______________ of many audiences with actors, film stars, athletes, and other famous people.

3. (illustrate) Many language textbooks include ______________ artwork and graphics.

4. (publish) Sales of hard copies of books are forecasted to decline as online ______________ of e-books increases.

5. (intervene) Police ______________ is often necessary in cases where domestic violence or child abuse is reported.

6. (seek) Einstein was right about many things and may have been wrong about some things. What is clear is that he always ______________ the truth.

Understanding Words in Context

Exercise 7: Words in Context

Complete each sentence with one of these words. Change the word form by adding *-s*, *-ed*, *-ize*, or *-tion*, or a combination of these, if necessary.

conform illustrate implicate insight summary target

1. Before agreeing to spray anything into the atmosphere, it is important to understand all environmental, financial, and health ____________ of such actions on global warming.

2. The 1960s was a decade when young adults did not wish to ____________ to the social rules established by their parents' generation.

3. These days, most TV reporters try to ____________ the news in as few words as possible.

4. Because of her good grades, high test scores, and impressive extra-curricular activities, she was ____________ by several companies before she graduated.

5. Meditation is not only recognized as a valuable tool for achieving relaxation and reducing stress. Many people claim that meditating gives them important ____________ into their own behavior and emotions.

6. Einstein ____________ his theory of relativity with mathematical equations and diagrams.

Exercise 8: Multiple Meanings of a Word/Parts of Speech

Several of the target words in this unit have more than one meaning. Read the sets of sentences, paying attention to the underlined word. Write N for noun or V for verb on the blank before each sentence. The word endings and word forms of all the words in a sentence can be used to help determine the parts of speech of other words. What word endings did you use as clues to help you determine the part of speech? For example, which words provided clues?

1. a. ____ Leo Tolstoy is the famous <u>author</u> of *War and Peace.*

   b. ____ Some Internet sites invite people to <u>author</u> short articles for payment or for royalties.

   Clues: ____

2. a. ____ Every year, many nonprofit organizations receive <u>grants</u> from the federal government to fund their work.

   b. ____ After his death, the rock star's family decided to <u>grant</u> a few interviews to the media.

   Clues: ____

3. a. ____ The Census is a sort of government <u>survey</u> that collects information such as how many people live in the districts of each state.

   b. ____ During the time just before elections, political parties usually <u>survey</u> people to find out which issues are most important to them.

   Clues: ____

4. a. ____ The military claims that it carefully tries to <u>target</u> terrorists and enemy forces when it carries out air strikes, but sometimes civilians are killed.

   b. ____ Children are the <u>target</u> of many marketing campaigns.

   Clues: ____

Using Words in Communication

Exercise 9: Reading

Read at least two short biographies of one of your favorite authors. You can find short biographies online or in reference books in the library. If you choose to find your information online, be sure you use reputable, legitimate sources. Write a short outline on a separate piece of paper or write notes on index cards. Include the information listed and any other interesting facts. Be prepared to share your information with the class.

- full name
- nationality (and countries the person lived in, if important)
- dates of birth and death
- names of major works
- things or people that influenced his or her work (if any are mentioned)
- brief personal information
- awards or honors received

Exercise 10: Writing

Write a three-paragraph summary of the plot of your favorite book by the author you researched in Exercise 9. Check one or more references to refresh your memory, if you need to, but be sure you do not plagiarize. Your summary must be your own words.

Exercise 11: Critical Thinking

These questions will help you develop your critical-thinking skills. Critical thinking helps you evaluate information and reach logical conclusions using the information that is given. Ask yourself the questions as you work on your answers: What information in the reading supports my answer? What other information do I have to support my conclusion? Where can I get more information about the topic?

First, answer the questions by yourself. Then share your answers with a partner. Decide on one answer for each question. Be prepared to explain your answers to the class.

1. According to the first reading in this unit, the MLA conducted a poll in which librarians were asked, "Which book should every adult read before they die?" What would your answer to this question be? Why?

2. Do you think novels are as important today as stories told in other media—for example in movies or in online blogs? Why or why not?

3. Several groups attempted to ban *To Kill a Mockingbird* from high school reading lists and from high school libraries. Do you think that a book dealing with the topic of rape should be banned? Do you think there is other content that should be banned in print or online? If yes, what? Defend your answer.

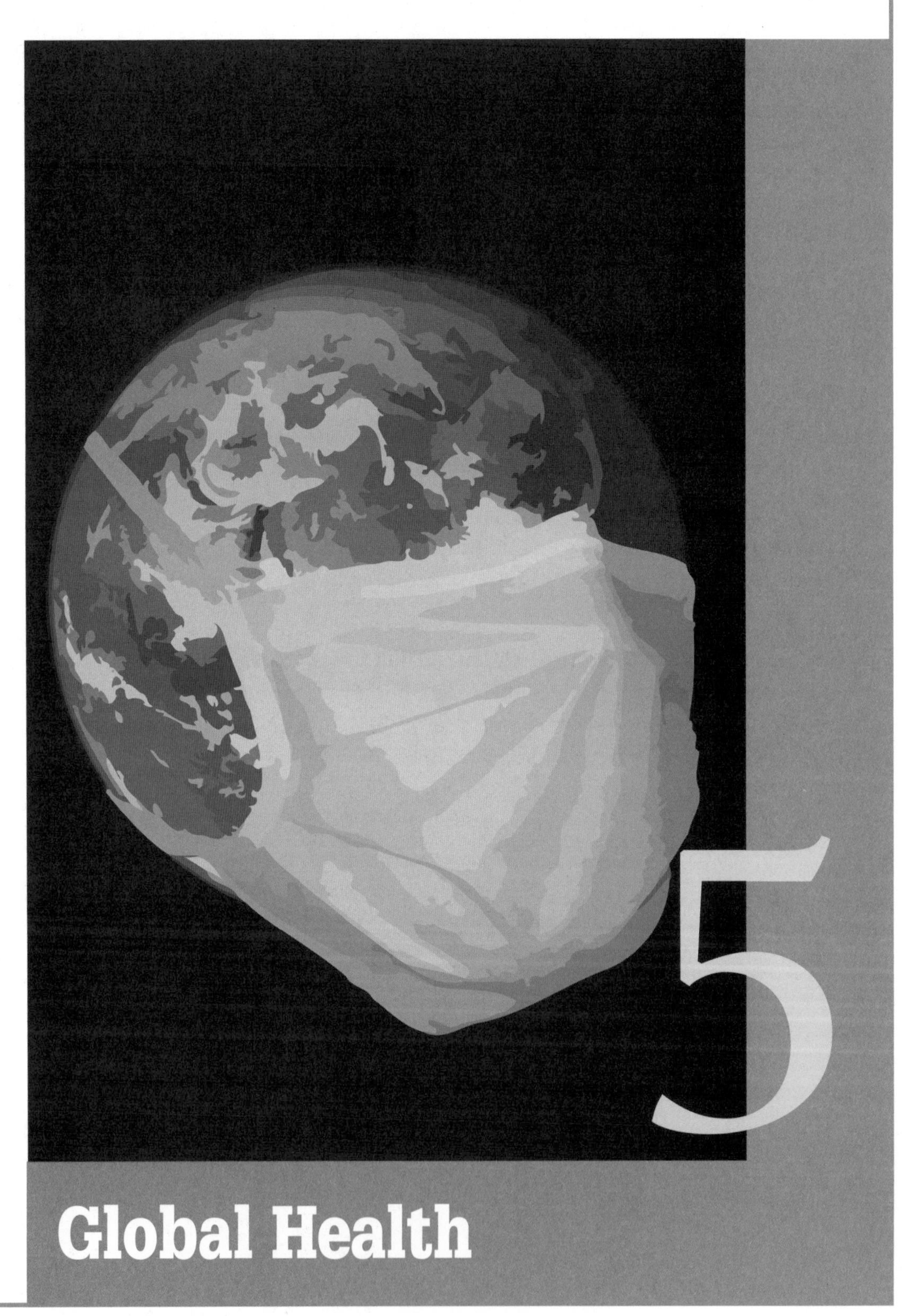

5

Global Health

Vocabulary Preview

Preview 1

These sentences contain information from the readings. Fill in the blanks with the word that best completes each sentence.

duration **dynamic** **emerged** **fluctuations** **incidence**

1. In the past 50 years, Hong Kong has reduced the ____________ of tuberculosis by almost 98 percent.

2. In many places, ____________ in temperature and rainfall can influence the numbers of disease-carrying rodents, such as rats and squirrels.

3. The ____________ of treatment for ordinary tuberculosis is six to eight months.

4. New infectious diseases, including Lyme disease, Legionnaire's disease, and hantavirus, have recently ____________ in the United States.

5. Microbes—viruses and bacteria—can develop resistance to drugs in an unpredictable and ____________ fashion.

Preview 2

Look at the way the underlined words are used in the sentences. Match each word with its meaning or definition.

1. Hantavirus was first detected in the southwestern United States in 1993.

2. In the first half of the 20th century, the number of cases of childhood diseases such as measles and whooping cough declined in the United States.

3. The use of antibiotic drugs, improved sanitation, and education all facilitate the treatment of tuberculosis in poor countries.

4. People with weak immune systems are more likely to develop active tuberculosis if they are exposed to TB bacteria.

5. One of the symptoms of tuberculosis is a persistent cough.

_____ 1. **detected**	a. enable something to happen easily
_____ 2. **declined**	b. discovered
_____ 3. **facilitate**	c. continuing, constant
_____ 4. **exposed**	d. put in a dangerous situation
_____ 5. **persistent**	e. lessened in quality

Reading Preview: What Do You Already Know?

Circle the correct answer. If you don't know the answer, guess.

1. All of these are examples of infectious diseases except
   a. tuberculosis
   b. whooping cough
   c. cancer
   d. malaria

2. The worldwide increase in the incidence of infectious diseases is mostly caused by
   a. the evolution of microbes
   b. the spread of human populations into tropical forests
   c. bacterial resistance to antibiotics
   d. all of the above

3. Since 2004, the largest number of new tuberculosis cases has emerged in
   a. Russia
   b. Southeast Asia
   c. Southern Africa
   d. The western United States

4. The normal course of treatment for tuberculosis is about
   a. 3–4 weeks
   b. 3–4 months
   c. 6–8 months
   d. 2 years

5. All of these statements about tuberculosis are true except
   a. All types of TB respond well to current drugs and treatment.
   b. TB can be diagnosed easily by testing the saliva of most TB patients.
   c. It is possible to be exposed to TB and not become sick until years later.
   d. The increase in numbers of TB is related to the epidemic of HIV/AIDS.

Introduction to the Readings

(1) New and re-emerging infectious diseases will pose a rising global health threat and will complicate U.S. and global security over the next 20 years. These diseases will endanger U.S. citizens at home and abroad, threaten U.S. armed forces deployed overseas, and exacerbate* social and political instability in key countries and regions in which the United States has significant interests.

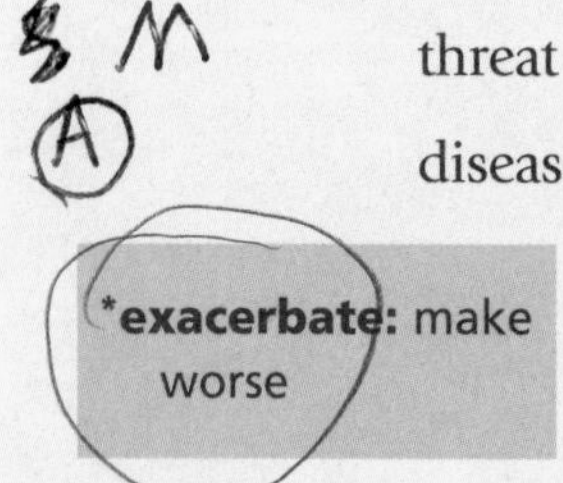

*exacerbate: make worse

(2) Infectious diseases are a leading cause of death, accounting for one-quarter to one-third of the estimated 54 million deaths worldwide annually. The spread of infectious diseases results as much from changes in human behavior—including lifestyles and land use patterns, increased trade and travel, and inappropriate use of antibiotic drugs—as from mutations in pathogens.* Of note:

*pathogens: tiny organisms that cause disease

- Twenty well-known diseases—including tuberculosis (TB), malaria, and cholera—have re-emerged or spread geographically since 1973, often in more virulent and drug-resistant forms. These are the leading killer infectious diseases on the planet, and they are spreading at an alarming rate because of the overuse and misuse of drugs that were supposed to cure them.
- At least 30 previously unknown disease agents have been identified since 1973, including HIV, Ebola, hepatitis C, and Nipah virus, for which no cures are available.
- Of the seven biggest killers worldwide, TB, malaria, hepatitis, and, in particular, HIV/AIDS continue to surge, with HIV/AIDS and TB likely to account for the overwhelming **majority** of deaths from infectious diseases in developing countries by 2020. Acute lower respiratory infections—including pneumonia and influenza—as well as diarrheal diseases and measles, appear to have peaked at high **incidence** levels.

(3) Reading 1 addresses some of the issues concerning emerging infectious diseases, including how a disease once thought to have been eradicated came back to threaten our global society: tuberculosis (or TB).

(4) Readings 2 and 3 focus on tuberculosis, a contagious airborne disease that spreads like a common cold and the dangers associated with trying to manage or cure it. TB is caused by a bacterium called *Mycobacterium tuberculosis* (or *M. tuberculosis*) that usually infects the lungs.

(5) TB is the top single infectious killer of adults worldwide: it will not **affect** one of every three people who have been **exposed,** but 10 percent will develop active TB, and 2 million people a year will die from it. For those individuals **exposed,** these infections can be re-activated years or even decades later if the immune system is weak. This explains why people living with HIV whose immune system has been suppressed by the virus are so vulnerable to TB.

(6) In the 1600s, TB was called the "great white plague" because it made people pale/white. Later it was called "consumption." By 1850, about 25 percent of Europeans and Americans died as a result of TB. Then in 1944, a miracle antibiotic cured a critically ill patient. More new drugs followed, and by the 1970s, it was assumed that the disease was a thing of the past.

(7) The pulmonary* form of TB is characterized by a **persistent** cough, shortness of breath and chest pain. Each person with the infectious form of TB, if untreated, will go on to infect between 10 and 15 other people each year. The *Mycobacterium* can also infect almost any part of the body, such as the lymph nodes, the spine, or bones. This is the extra-pulmonary form of TB and is more common in HIV-infected patients and children. Although extra-pulmonary TB may not be contagious, it is equally vital to diagnose and treat rapidly, as all forms of the disease can be deadly if adequate treatment is not received.

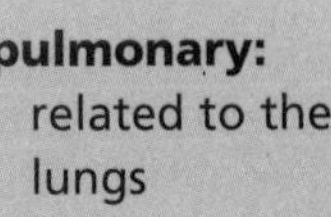

***pulmonary:** related to the lungs

(8) People infected with both TB and HIV often present unclear clinical symptoms and are frequently missed by existing diagnostic tools. The most

widely used technique for diagnosing TB in developing countries is no more sophisticated than examining a suspected patient's sputum* sample under a microscope to assess whether it contains *TB mycobacteria*. This method, called sputum-smear microscopy, was developed more than a century ago.

***sputum:** as used here, a sample of someone's spit (or saliva)

(9) Although relatively fast and easy to implement in resource-limited settings, the method has significant limitations: it **detects** less than half of all TB cases, and it is, by definition, not able to identify TB in people, such as children or many people living with HIV, who either have difficulties producing enough sputum from their lungs for a sample for analysis or don't have sufficient or any *mycobacteria* in their sputum to be **detected** under the microscope. It also completely misses the extra-pulmonary form of TB.

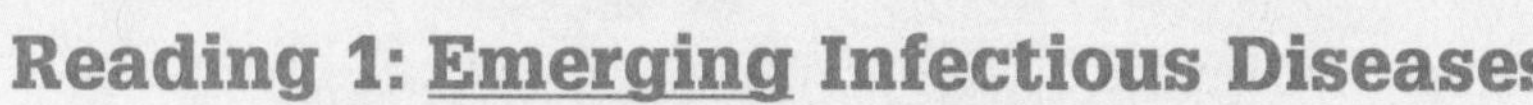

Reading 1: Emerging Infectious Diseases

Excerpt adapted and updated from
Preventing Emerging Infectious Diseases: A Strategy for the 21st Century
(Atlanta: Center for Disease Control, 1998).

(10) Forty years ago, the threat of infectious diseases appeared to be receding. Modern scientific advances—including antibiotic drugs, vaccines against childhood diseases, and improved technology for sanitation—had **facilitated** the control or prevention of many infectious diseases, particularly in industrialized nations. The **incidence** of childhood diseases such as polio, whooping cough, and diphtheria was **declining** due to the use of vaccines. In addition, American physicians had fast-acting, effective antibiotics to combat often-fatal bacterial diseases such as meningitis and pneumonia. Deaths from infection, commonplace at the beginning of the 20th century, were no longer a frequent occurrence in the United States. Meanwhile, in other parts of the world, chemical pesticides like DDT were lowering the **incidence** of malaria, a **major** killer of children, by controlling populations of parasite-carrying mosquitoes.

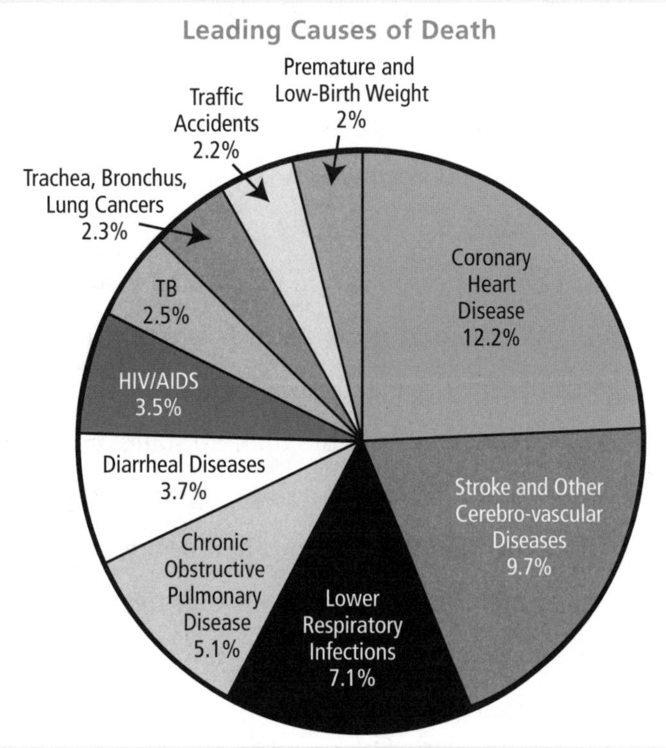

Data from the World Health Organization, 2009

(11) As it turned out, that euphoria* was premature. It did not take into account the extraordinary resilience of infectious microbes,* which have a remarkable ability to evolve, adapt, and develop resistance to drugs in an unpredictable and **dynamic** fashion. It also did not take into account the accelerating spread of human populations into tropical forests and overcrowded mega-cities where people are **exposed** to a variety of emerging infectious agents.

***euphoria:** happy excitement

***microbes:** germs, bacteria viruses too small to be seen without a microscope

(12) Today, most health professionals agree that new microbial threats are appearing in significant numbers, while well-known illnesses thought to be under control are re-emerging. Most Americans are aware of the epidemic of the acquired immunodeficiency syndrome (AIDS) and the related increase in tuberculosis (TB) cases in the United States. In fact, there has been a general resurgence of infectious diseases throughout the world, including significant

outbreaks of cholera, malaria, yellow fever, and diphtheria. In addition, bacterial resistance to antibiotic drugs is an increasingly serious worldwide problem. For example, the Ebola virus, which causes an often-fatal illness, appeared in Africa, and a formerly unknown virus of the measles family that killed several horses in Australia also infected humans.

(13) New diseases also appeared within the United States, including Lyme disease, Legionnaires' disease, and more recently hantavirus pulmonary syndrome (HPS). HPS was first recognized in the southwestern United States in 1993 and has since been **detected** in more than 20 states and in several other countries in the Americas. Other new or re-emerging threats in the United States include multidrug-resistant TB; antibiotic-resistant bacteria causing ear infections; pneumonia; meningitis; rabies; and diarrheal diseases caused by the parasite *Cryptosporidium parvum* and by certain toxigenic strains of *Escherichia coli** bacteria.

Escherichia coli: called e-coli in the news

(14) Why are new infectious diseases emerging?

(15) The reasons for the sharp increase in **incidence** of many infectious diseases once thought to be under control are **complex** and not fully understood. Population shifts and population growth; changes in human behavior; urbanization, poverty, and crowding; changes in ecology and climate; the evolution of microbes; inadequacy of public health infrastructures; and modern travel and trade have all contributed. For example, the ease of modern travel creates many opportunities for a disease outbreak in remote areas to spread to a crowded urban area. Human behavioral factors, such as dietary habits and food handling, personal hygiene, risky sexual behavior, and intravenous drug use, can contribute to disease emergence. In several parts of the world, human encroachment on tropical forests has brought populations with little or no disease resistance into close proximity with insects that carry malaria and yellow fever and other, sometimes unknown, infectious diseases. In addition, local **fluctuations** in temperature and rainfall **affect** the number

In some big cities, people wear masks to help reduce the spread of TB and other infectious diseases.

of microbe-carrying rodents in some areas. Finally, in many parts of the world there has been a deterioration in the local public health infrastructures that monitor and respond to disease outbreaks.

Reading 2: Tuberculosis in the Western Pacific Region

Excerpt adapted and updated from *Voice of America* report March 19, 2007, by Heda Bayron, "WHO Calls for Urgent Action Against Multi-Drug Resistant TB in Asia-Pacific." Voanews.com.

(16) About two million people in the Western Pacific region, including Cambodia, China, Laos, Mongolia, Papua New Guinea, the Philippines and Vietnam, develop TB each year. Poverty, an aging population, and rising HIV infections are helping spread the respiratory disease. And now health experts in Asia are **stressing** the urgency of controlling an even bigger **medical** threat: drug-resistant tuberculosis.

(17) Drug resistance means that the drugs normally used to kill the TB bacteria lose their effectiveness and stop working. Resistance occurs most commonly when patients stop taking their **medication** before completing the full course of therapy. The weaker strains of the bacterium get killed off during treatment, leaving the stronger and more resistant ones to replicate and flourish once the **medication** is discontinued. Other factors contributing to drug resistance include poor-quality drugs; lack of drug availability, especially in remote or developing areas; and prescribing the wrong drug, the wrong dose, or the wrong **duration** of treatment.

(18) TB that is resistant to at least two of the most commonly used anti-TB drugs is known as "multi-drug resistant TB," or MDR-TB. Unlike ordinary TB—which can be cured by antibiotics within six to eight months—MDR-TB requires more powerful and expensive drugs taken for more than two years, often with severe side effects including loss of hearing, vomiting, dizziness, and more. In 2009, U.S. health officials identified an "extremely drug-resistant TB," called XX-DR, a very rare strain that was starting to cause concern.

(19) According to the World Health Organization, more than a quarter of the world's multi-drug resistant cases are found in the Western Pacific. A **majority** of them—around 140,000 cases in 2007—are concentrated in China.

(20) Dr. Pieter van Maaren, head of the Stop TB department of the WHO in the Western Pacific, says the emergence of MDR-TB can be blamed on a failure to implement the standard treatment strategy known as DOTS, or "direct observed treatment short course."

(21) "It's a man-made problem," says van Maaren. "What you see in China for example is that in the past, the TB-control program was not very strong and China [did not manage] TB patients according to the DOTS strategy. . . . [I]t was only in 2002, 2003 that the entire country had access to DOTS strategy—the best way of managing TB. That is why we see at this point in time the problem of drug-resistant TB in China emerging."

(22) DOTS combats the problem of drug resistance by requiring patients to come to clinics daily or several times a week to take their medicines. There, health workers closely monitor correct dosage and **duration** of treatment.

(23) In Hong Kong, where the fight against TB and drug resistance has been successful, anti-TB drugs are given free in public clinics. Because of the city's size, patients have easy access to them. In the past 50 years, Hong Kong has reduced its **incidence** of TB by almost 98 percent.

(24) But, says Dr. S.L. Chan, a tuberculosis expert at the Hong Kong Tuberculosis, Chest and Heart Disease Association, getting patients to stay on course with DOTS is a multi-faceted challenge.

(25) "In the past you [could] say, 'You must have treatment,' and they [had] no choice," said Dr. Chan. "But now because of human rights, if you tell them, 'You must have DOTS,' they will say, 'I can't.' You can't force them. Another thing, in Hong Kong there is still a large proportion of the population suffering from tuberculosis in the age between 20–49. They are the working group. How can they come to the clinic for supervised treatment?"

(26) Other challenges include funding and reaching people in remote areas or places with overtaxed health **facilities**.

(27) The Western Pacific sees two million TB cases develop each year, and more than 800 people die from the respiratory illness every day.

(28) The WHO has set an ambitious goal for the whole region, and that is to cut by half TB prevalence and mortality by 2012.

(29) Doctors say the region's rising HIV/AIDS epidemic, **persistent** poverty, and dismal public health funding are the main obstacles to these goals.

(30) The WHO is urging governments in Asia to invest in immediate action. The problem, however, is that stopping the more virulent strains of the disease is costlier and more **complex**.

(31) The WHO says the region has only earmarked less than 10 percent of the nearly one billion dollars it needs to combat the disease through 2012. More than 200 million of it would be needed to contain multi-drug resistant TB.

Reading 3: Chart of Latent TB Infection and TB Disease

Excerpt from Centers for Disease Control, Division of Tuberculosis (www.cdc.gov/tb/publications/factseries/cure_eng.htm); accessed January 10, 2010.

*latent: present but inactive

(32) Two TB-related conditions exist: latent* TB infection and active TB disease. As a result, not everyone infected with TB bacteria becomes sick.

Latent TB Infection

(33) TB bacteria can live in your body without making you sick. This is called *latent TB infection* (LTBI). In most people who breathe in TB bacteria and become infected, the body is able to fight the bacteria to stop them from growing. People with latent TB infection do not feel sick and do not have any symptoms. The only sign of TB infection is a positive **reaction** to the tuberculin skin test or special TB blood test. People with latent TB infection are not infectious and cannot spread TB bacteria to others. However, if TB bacteria become active in the body and multiply, the person will get sick with TB disease.

TB Disease

(34) TB bacteria become active if the immune system can't stop them from growing. When TB bacteria are active (multiplying in your body), this is called *TB disease*. TB disease will make you sick. People with TB disease may spread the bacteria to people they spend time with every day. Some people develop TB disease soon after becoming infected (within weeks), before their immune system can fight the TB bacteria. Other people may get sick years later, when their immune system becomes weak for another reason.

(35) For persons whose immune systems are weak, especially those with HIV infection, the risk of developing TB disease is much higher than for persons with normal immune systems.

The Difference between Latent TB Infection and TB Disease	
A Person with Latent TB Infection	**A Person with TB Disease**
• Has no symptoms	• Has symptoms that may include: —a bad cough that lasts 3 weeks or longer —pain in the chest —coughing up blood or sputum —weakness or fatigue —weight loss —no appetite —chills —fever —sweating at night
• Does not feel sick	• Usually feels sick
• Cannot spread TB bacteria to others	• May spread TB bacteria to others
• Usually has a skin test or blood test result indicating TB infection	• Usually has a skin test or blood test result indicating TB infection
• Has a normal chest x-ray and a negative sputum smear	• May have an abnormal chest x-ray or positive sputum smear or culture
• Needs treatment for latent TB infection to prevent active TB disease	• Needs treatment to treat active TB disease

Comprehension Check

Did you understand the readings? Mark these sentences true (T) or false (F).

_____ 1. In the second half of the 20th century, deaths from infection were rare in the United States.

_____ 2. Malaria is spread through the air by bacteria.

_____ 3. So far, hantavirus has been detected only in Africa.

_____ 4. New infectious diseases are likely to be discovered as people move into or closer to tropical rain forests.

_____ 5. Most often, drug resistance in TB patients is caused by a shortage of drugs in remote areas.

_____ 6. The treatment for drug-resistant TB is more expensive than the treatment for ordinary TB.

_____ 7. Approximately 25 percent of the world's multi-drug resistant cases of TB are found in the Western Pacific.

_____ 8. In the DOTS treatment program for TB, family members directly observe patients taking their medicine.

_____ 9. Hong Kong has worked hard over the past 50 years and has almost eliminated TB as a health concern.

_____ 10. In patients with latent tuberculosis, the disease is not active, but the patients are still infectious.

Word Study

Target Vocabulary

affect
complex
decline
detect
duration
dynamic
expose
facilitate
fluctuate (fluctuations)
incidence
major (majority)
medical
persist (persistent)
react (reaction)
stress

Word Parts

Scan the readings for these words with an *re-* prefix. The prefix *re-* comes from Latin and means "again," "back," or "against." It is used to form many English words.

Exercise 1: Prefixes

Find these words in the readings. Using the context and the chart, write a definition for each word.

1. **receding:** ______________________
2. **resilience:** ______________________
3. **resistant:** ______________________
4. **resurgence:** ______________________
5. **reduced:** ______________________

When attached to an existing English word[1], the prefix *re-* means "again." Think about these root words preceded by *re-*. Define and then write a sentence using each word.

1. **re-emerge** ______________________

   ____

2. **re-expose** ______________________

   ____

3. **re-infect** ______________________

   ____

4. **re-occur** ______________________

   ____

5. **re-create** ______________________

   ____

Can you think of other words that use *re-* this way? List them.

____

____

____

[1] Often, but not always, *re-* is followed by a hyphen; contrast *re-emerge* versus *rewrite*.

Exercise 2: The Roots

The root *-dur-* comes from the Latin word *durare*, meaning "to last, harden." Study some of the English words that come from this root. Then use the words to fill in the blanks in the sentences.

Noun	*duration*
Verb	*endure*
Adjective	*durable*
Adverb	*during*

1. The ______________ of treatment for multidrug-resistant TB can be as long as two years.

2. The young woman was stricken with polio and had to ______________ years of painful and difficult treatments.

3. The influenza virus is most active ______________ the winter months.

4. Today it is possible to build health clinics in remote areas with inexpensive and ______________ materials such as bamboo and clay.

The root *-facil-* comes from the Latin word *facere* and originally meant "to do." Over time, it has come to have the meaning "easy to do." Study the English words that come from this root. Then use the words to fill in the blanks in the sentences.

Noun	*facility*
Noun (a person)	*facilitator*
Verb	*facilitate*
Adjective	*facile*

1. Marcia has a ________________ for languages. She already speaks five and is learning two more.

2. The conference organizers hired a ________________ to introduce the speakers and guide the discussions.

3. That is a complicated problem. We must not use a ________________ solution.

4. You can ________________ the writing process if you make an outline first.

Word Relationships

Exercise 3 : Commonly Confused Words

The words *affect* and *effect* sound alike, but they are used in very different ways. Study the definitions of the two words. Then fill in the blanks in the sentences with the correct word.

affect [transitive verb] 1. to influence somebody or something; to have an effect on. 2. to move somebody emotionally

effect [noun] 1. a result; a changed condition occurring as a result of action by somebody or something else. 2. an impression in the mind of someone who sees, hears, or reads something.

Usage
Generally, *affect* is used as a verb, while *effect* most often is used as a noun. If one thing *affects* (acts on) another, it *has an effect* on it (causes it to change). *The hot weather* ***affected*** *everyone's mood. One effect of global warming is rising sea levels. Music has a calming* ***effect*** *on young children.*

1. Changes in temperature and rainfall can _______________ the number of disease-carrying rodents in some areas.

2. What _______________ does exposure to loud noise have on the ability of young children to learn?

3. Advertising has a powerful _______________ on people's opinions, even if they don't realize it.

4. How will warmer oceans _______________ sea life?

5. The president's speech about health care did not _______________ most people's opinions one way or the other.

The Grammar of Words and Word Families

Exercise 4: Word Families

Use these words to fill in the word family chart. Some words will be used more than once.

affect (2x)

complex (2x)
complexity

decline (2x)

detect
detectable
detectability
detection
detective
detector (2x)

duration
durable
durability

dynamic (2x)
dynamically

expose
exposability
exposable
exposed
exposition
exposure

facilitate
facilitation
facilitative
facilitator
facility

fluctuate
fluctuation

incidence
incident
incidental
incidentally

majority
major (4x)

medical
medically
medicate
medicine

persist
persistence
persistency
persistent
persistently

react
reaction
reactive
reactor (2x)

stress (2x)
stressful
stressor

Noun	Noun (person)	Verb	Adjective	Adverb
	—	affect	—	
	—	—	complex	—
	—	decline	—	—
		detect		—
duration	—	—		—
	—	—	dynamic	
	—	expose		
		facilitate		—
	—	fluctuate		—
incidence	—	—		
majority				—
	—		medical	
	—		persistent	
	—	react		—
stress	—			—

Exercise 5: Word Forms

Complete each sentence with the correct form of the word in parentheses. Add prefixes and suffixes as necessary, and follow spelling rules.

1. (decline) The school was closed because of ________________ enrollment.

2. (majority) Malaria, a ________________ killer of children, can be controlled by pesticides such as DDT.

3. (medical) Under the DOTS system, tuberculosis patients are not allowed to ________________ themselves.

4. (persistent) In spite of new laws passed by the legislature, our economic problems ________________.

5. (reaction) Although Sarah was deeply hurt by her husband's words, she did not ________________.

6. (stress) Overcrowding is one of the most ________________ aspects of living in mega-cities like Mumbai, Mexico City, and Beijing.

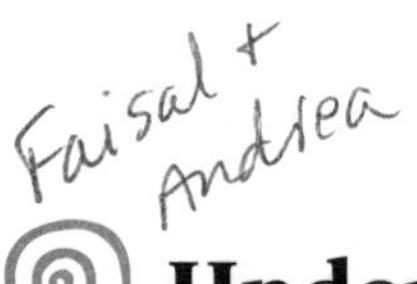

Understanding Words in Context

Exercise 6: Participial Phrases

Some adjective clauses can be reduced to phrases. The phrases are then placed before the nouns they modify. For example:

mosquitoes that carry parasites ←→ parasite-carrying mosquitoes

Pesticides like DDT are used to lower the ***incidence*** *of malaria, a* ***major*** *killer of children, by controlling populations of parasite-carrying mosquitoes.*

Change the clauses into phrases. Then write a sentence containing each phrase. Consult the readings if necessary.

1. a population that is declining ______________________________

   ____

2. a threat that is receding ______________________________

   ____

3. nations that are industrializing ______________________________

   ____

4. antibiotics that act fast ______________________________

   ____

5. a problem that is re-emerging ______________________________

   ____

Exercise 7: Word Meanings in Context

Look at the way the underlined words are used in the passages, the context given for each. Then match each word with its meaning or definition.

1. As it turns out, our understandable euphoria was premature. It did not take into account the extraordinary resilience of microbes, which have a remarkable ability to evolve, adapt, and develop resistance to drugs in an unpredictable and dynamic fashion.

2. In several parts of the world, human encroachment on tropical forests has brought populations with little or no disease resistance into close proximity with insects that carry malaria and yellow fever.

_____ 1. euphoria	a. tiny living organisms, especially those that cause disease
_____ 2. take into account	b. the act of trespassing or intruding into a limited or forbidden area
_____ 3. microbes	c. closeness in time or space
_____ 4. encroachment	d. consider
_____ 5. proximity	e. feeling of great happiness

Exercise 8: Examples as Context Clues

Read the sentences from the readings. Notice the expressions that are used to signal examples. Then use the examples to guess the meanings of the underlined words. Write definitions in the spaces.

1. The incidence of <u>childhood diseases</u> such as polio, whooping cough, and diphtheria was declining due to the use of vaccines.

2. In other parts of the world, chemical <u>pesticides</u> like DDT were lowering the incidence of malaria.

3. Human <u>behavioral factors</u>, such as dietary habits and food handling, personal hygiene, risky sexual behavior, and intravenous drug use, can contribute to disease emergence.

4. MDR-TB requires more powerful and expensive drugs taken for more than two years, often with severe <u>side effects</u> including loss of hearing, vomiting, dizziness, and more.

5. A person with TB disease has <u>symptoms</u> that may include a bad cough, pain in the chest, weakness, weight loss, chills, fever, and sweating at night.

a. childhood diseases ______________________________

b. pesticides ______________________________

c. behavioral factors ______________________________

d. side effects ______________________________

e. symptoms ______________________________

Exercise 9: Words with Multiple Meanings

In each sentence, the underlined word has multiple meanings. Read the sentences. Then find the words in your dictionary, and copy the definition that matches the way the words are used.

1. American physicians had fast-acting, effective antibiotics to combat often-fatal bacterial diseases.

   combat: ____________________

   ____

2. It also did not take into account the accelerating spread of human populations into tropical forests and overcrowded mega-cities where people are exposed to a variety of emerging infectious agents.

   agents: ____________________

   ____

3. The problem is that stopping the more virulent strains of the disease is costlier and more complex.

   complex: ____________________

   ____

4. Health experts in Asia are stressing the urgency of controlling an even bigger medical threat: drug-resistant tuberculosis.

   stress(ing): ____________________

   ____

5. A person with active TB may have an abnormal chest x-ray or positive sputum smear or culture.

   culture: ____________________

   ____

Exercise 10: Noun-Preposition Collocations

Scan the readings to find the first occurence of the words used as nouns. Then copy the preposition—*in*, *of*, or *to*—and the object following each noun. Follow the example.

1. incidence ____
2. fluctuations ____
3. majority ____
4. emergence ____
5. duration ____
6. reaction ____

Use each collocation in an original sentence.

1. ____
2. ____
3. ____
4. ____
5. ____
6. ____

Using Words in Communication

Exercise 11: Reading

Select one of the infectious diseases listed, and do research to answer the questions on a separate sheet of paper.

cholera	**malaria**	**yellow fever**
swine flu (H1N1 virus)	**diphtheria**	**measles**
Lyme disease	**Legionnaire's disease**	**Ebola**
polio	**whooping cough**	**meningitis**

1. What is the disease? What causes it? What are the symptoms?

2. Where is the disease prevalent? Who is most affected by it?

3. What is the treatment? Is the disease curable?

4. What special problems (such as drug resistance) are associated with this disease? What steps are health officials taking to address these problems?

Exercise 12: Speaking or Writing

Using your notes prepare a 5–7 minute oral report about the disease you researched. In your presentation include at least one visual aid, such as a diagram or chart. If your teacher prefers, write a 3–5 page report about the disease you researched. Include diagrams and charts.

Exercise 13: Critical Thinking

These questions will help you develop your critical-thinking skills. Critical thinking helps you evaluate information and reach good conclusions using the information that is given. Ask yourself the questions as you work on your answers: What information in the readings support my answer? What other information do I have to support my conclusion? Where can I get more information about the topic?

1. Discuss how each of these factors might affect the emergence or re-emergence of infectious diseases:
   - urbanization
   - climate change
   - poverty versus wealth of individuals and the country as a whole
   - travel and trade
   - movement of humans into previously uninhabited areas, such as rain forests
   - personal behavior
2. Is tuberculosis a significant problem in the country or area where you live? If yes, how is the government addressing the problem?
3. Is DOTS used in your area or country? Why or why not?
4. In your opinion, how should these agencies help to prevent communicable diseases:
   - international bodies such as the World Health Organization
   - government agencies or ministries
   - schools
   - parents

6 Conserving National Resources

Vocabulary Preview

Preview 1

These sentences contain information from the readings. Fill in the blanks with the word that best completes each sentence.

expansion funding impose precedent restore

1. George Catlin, the inventor of the national park concept, was worried about the impact of American's westward ________________ on Native Indian civilization.

2. One of the responsibilities of the National Park Service is to preserve and ________________ historic monuments.

3. Americans have always been willing to ________________ legal limits on their own use of public lands in order to preserve them for future generations.

4. Yellowstone was the first public land area designated as a national park. Following this ________________, Congress soon set aside Yosemite, Mount Rainier, Crater Lake, and other areas for the same purpose.

5. These days, the greatest concern among conservationists is how to find new sources of ________________ for its projects.

Preview 2

Look at the way the underlined words are used in the sentences. Match each word with its meaning or definition.

1. Where will the money for conservation initiatives come from in the coming decades?

2. The Wetlands Reserve Program pays farmers and ranchers to conserve habitat and prevent erosion.

3. Plants and animals cannot survive without an adequate supply of food and water.

4. The efforts of private companies to promote "green" habits among their employees complement the government's efforts to encourage people to conserve and recycle.

5. If people act now, we still have the potential to reduce some of the negative effects of global warming.

_____ 1. **initiatives**	a. gradual destruction, especially of soil
_____ 2. **erosion**	b. something that completes or perfects something else
_____ 3. **adequate**	c. possibility
_____ 4. **complement**	d. enough
_____ 5. **potential**	e. plan or strategy for dealing with a problem

Reading Preview: What Do You Already Know?

Circle the correct answer. If you don't know the answer, guess.

1. The National Park Service was established between
   a. 1830–1840
   b. 1910–1920
   c. 1930–1940
   d. 1950–1960

2. All of these are national parks except
   a. The Grand Canyon
   b. Yosemite
   c. Yankee Stadium
   d. Mammoth Cave

3. The National Park Service is not responsible for
   a. national parks
   b. historic monuments
   c. battlefields
   d. interstate highways

4. The earliest conservation efforts in America were initiated by
   a. hunters
   b. commercial fishermen
   c. the federal government
   d. cattle ranchers

5. The U.S. president generally considered to be the greatest conservation president was
   a. Abraham Lincoln (1860–1865)
   b. Teddy Roosevelt (1901–1909)
   c. Franklin Delano Roosevelt (1933–1945)
   d. Gerald Ford (1974–1977)

Introduction to the Readings

(1) Officially, the U.S. National Park System began in 1872 when President Ulysses S. Grant signed the law that set aside the land in Yellowstone National Park to be protected by the U.S. government. Today the National Park System represents more than 450 natural, historical, recreational, and cultural areas. The system includes national parks, national monuments (like the Washington Monument or Statue of Liberty), national memorials (like Arlington National Cemetery), national military parks (like Gettysburg), national historic sites (like Independence Hall), national parkways (like Blue Ridge, which begins in Virginia and goes through North Carolina), national recreational areas (like Culee Dam in the Lake Roosevelt National Recreation Area), national seashores (like Cape Cod), national scenic riverways (like the Ozarks), national scenic trails (like the Cuyahoga Valley National Park Trails in Ohio), and others. The most recent addition to the list of national parks is a military base in Northern California on the Sacramento River. In December 2009, President Obama signed legislation making the Port Chicago Naval Magazine National Memorial a fully recognized part of the national park system. The site commemorates a July 17, 1944 explosion that killed 320 sailors and blew ships out of the water.

(2) Reading 1 provides a good overview of the origin of the public park concept, something that has often been called "America's best idea." In his 2009 PBS documentary *The National Parks*, filmmaker Ken Burns links the idea of the parks with the Declaration of Independence: "For the first time in human history, land—great sections of our natural landscape—was set aside, not for kings or noblemen or the very rich, but for everyone, for all time."

(3) Reading 2, from a textbook, also focuses on the history but offers some perspective on the costs associated with preserving the national parks and with land conservation* in general.

***conservation:** protection of nature

Reading 1: The National Park Is Born

Excerpt adapted from www.nps.gov/history/history/hisnps/NPSHistory/briefhistory.htm, accessed January 10, 2010.

Old Faithful is one of the most popular attractions at Yellowstone National Park.

(4) The national park concept is generally credited to the artist George Catlin. On a trip to the Dakotas in 1832, he worried about the impact of America's westward **expansion** on Native American civilization, wildlife, and wilderness. They might be preserved, he wrote, "by some great protecting policy of government . . . in a magnificent park. . . . A nation's park, containing man and beast, in all the wild and freshness of their nature's beauty."

(5) Catlin's vision was partly realized in 1864, when Congress donated Yosemite Valley to California for preservation as a state park. Eight years later, in 1872, Congress reserved the spectacular Yellowstone County in the Wyoming and Montana territories "as a public park or pleasuring-ground for the benefit and enjoyment of the people." With no state government there yet to receive and manage it, Yellowstone remained in the custody of the U.S. Department of the Interior as a national park—the world's first area so designated.

(6) Congress followed the Yellowstone **precedent** with other national parks in the 1890s and early 1900s, including Sequoia, Yosemite, Mount Rainier, Crater Lake, and Glacier. The idealistic impulse to preserve nature was often joined by the pragmatic desire to promote tourism: Western railroads lobbied for many of the early parks and built grand rustic hotels in them to boost their passenger business.

(7) By 1916 the Department of the Interior was responsible for 14 national parks and 21 national monuments but had no organization to manage them. Interior staff had asked the Army to send troops to Yellowstone and the California parks for this purpose. There, military engineers and cavalrymen developed park roads and buildings and enforced regulations against hunting, grazing, timber cutting, and vandalism. They did their best to serve the visiting public. Civilian appointees managed the other parks, while the monuments received minimal care.

(8) On August 25, 1916, President Woodrow Wilson approved legislation creating the National Park Service within the Department of the Interior. A new policy was established on the basis that more visitors must be attracted and accommodated if the parks were to survive. Automobiles, not permitted in Yellowstone until 1915, would be allowed throughout the system. Hotels would be provided. Museums, publications, and other educational activities were encouraged as well.

(9) The policy letter also made a **commitment** to **expanding** the system. Through the 1920s the national park system was really a western park system. The West was home to the United States' most spectacular natural scenery, and most land there was federally owned and was subject to park or monument reservation without purchase. If the system were to benefit more people and maximize its support in Congress, however, it would have to **expand** eastward. In 1926 Congress authorized Shenandoah, Great Smoky Mountains, and Mammoth Cave national parks in the Appalachian region but required that their lands be donated.

(10) The Park Service's greatest opportunity in the East lay in another realm—that of history and historic sites. Congress had directed the War Department* to preserve and **restore** a number of historic battlefields, forts, and memorials as national military parks and monuments, beginning in 1890 with Chickamauga and Chattanooga National Military Park in Georgia and Tennessee. . . .

***War Department:** now the named Department of Defense

(11) The addition of nearly 50 historical areas in the East under President Franklin D. Roosevelt made the park system and Park Service a truly national one and deeply involved with historic as well as natural preservation.

(12) During the 1930s the Park Service also became involved with areas intended primarily for recreation. In 1936, under an agreement with the Bureau of Reclamation, the Park Service assumed responsibility for recreational development and activities at the vast reservoir* created by Hoover Dam. In 1937 Congress authorized Cape Hatteras National Seashore, the first of several seashore and lakeshore areas.

***reservoir:** a supply of something, often water

(13) In 1951 a ten-year, billion-dollar program to upgrade facilities, staffing, and resource management by the Park Service's 50th anniversary in 1966 was instituted. By 1960, 56 visitor centers were open or under construction.

(14) During the bicentennial of the American Revolution in the mid-1970s, the two dozen historical parks commemorating the Revolution benefited from another big development program. On July 4, 1976, President Gerald R. Ford, once a **ranger** at Yellowstone, spoke at Independence Hall and signed legislation making Valley Forge a national historical park.

(15) Four years later, the Alaska National Interest Lands Conservation Act of 1980 more than doubled the size of the national park system by adding more than 47 million wilderness acres. The largest of the new areas in Alaska, Wrangell-St. Elias National Park, comprises more than 8,300,000 acres, while the adjoining Wrangell-St. Elias National Preserve comprises nearly 4,900,000.

(16) In recent years Park **expansion** has slowed as the government directed more money to the improvement of pre-existing parks. By this time the national park system comprised some 370 areas in nearly every state and U.S. possession.

(17) Public opinion surveys consistently rated the National Park Service among the most popular federal agencies. The high regard in which the national parks and their custodians were held augured* well for philanthropic, **corporate,** and volunteer support, present from the beginnings of the national park movement but never more vital to its prosperity.

***augured:** was a predictor of

Reading 2: The Costs of Preserving Natural Resources

Excerpt adapted from *From Walden to Wall Street: Frontiers of Conservation Finance,* edited by James N. Levitt (Washington DC: Island Press, 2005), pp. xi–xv. Copyright 2005 Lincoln Institute of Land Policy.

(18) Americans have practiced conservation for centuries. From the Puritans' protection of Boston Common in New England to the exemplary landscape stewardship* practiced by George Washington and Thomas Jefferson in Virginia, conservation has been a part of American culture since the founding of the nation. As a broad political movement, how-

***stewardship:** management or responsibility for

ever, conservation started coming into its own and taking on a national character in the mid-nineteenth century. Among several conservation-related **initiatives** of the era, one of the most important was the effort mounted by sportsmen, in response to the ravages of commercial hunting, to establish seasons and limits as well as formal means of enforcing such restrictions. Their aim, concisely stated, was to sustainably manage wild game (deer, ducks). That simple conservation philosophy, based on the belief that we Americans need to constructively **restrain** ourselves to **ensure** that resources like game animals will be available for future generations, became an important model for the subsequent management of natural resources throughout the country.

(19) In the centuries since, the ideals of the American conservation movement have found their expression in numerous tangible* ways. Much has been achieved during that time through the enactment of legal restrictions on the exploitation of natural resources. But the willingness of society to **impose** legal limitations on its use of land, water, fish, and game has been only a part of the story. In public, private, and philanthropic capacities, Americans have repeatedly shown a willingness to **commit** ingenuity and money to the constructive conservation of our natural resources.

***tangible:** perceptible by touch

(20) Indeed, the successful conservation of our nation's natural resources ultimately depends on the timely and **adequate commitment** of human and financial resources to get the job done. In America's free market economy, where citizens and policy makers balance the rights of property owners to utilize their private lands against the need to protect essentially public resources such as wildlife, conservationists must often bid against competing purposes to protect natural resources.

(21) Fortunately, conservationists, **ranging** from local activists to U.S. presidents, have fought in the political arena to secure the investment of federal and state monies in the cause of protecting natural resources. At the same time, philanthropic enterprises such as local land trusts have sprung up,

President Theodore Roosevelt made many speeches in favor of preserving land.

complementing and leveraging public investments to **expand** conservation efforts. Examples of conservation investments by the private, non-profit, and public sectors are everywhere, in every state in the country.

(22) Both in quantity and quality, much of the most significant conserved land is held by the federal government. The acquisition, maintenance, and management of these federal lands, including the national wildlife refuges, the national forests, and the national parks, were greatly advanced by President Theodore Roosevelt. The conservation work for which he laid much of the groundwork continues to this day and has required the public investment of tens of billions of dollars.

(23) The wide recognition of Teddy Roosevelt [President from 1901 to 1909] as America's greatest conservation president is, in great measure, based on an understanding of his passionate love for the outdoors. Through his words and deeds, Roosevelt was instrumental in defining the American

sportsman/conservationist ethic that we know today. As a politician and national leader, Roosevelt understood that the conservation ethic must be backed up with **adequate** funding for resource management. He fought long and hard for the establishment of state and federal agencies that would set the standard for many decades to come.

(24) Presidents and Congresses that followed built on the foundation laid by Theodore Roosevelt and his associates. Theodore's younger kinsman, Franklin Roosevelt [President from 1933 to 1945] , signed into law in 1937 the Pittman-Robertson Act. With the enthusiastic support of hunters and fishermen, this legislation continues to direct excise taxes on hunting and fishing equipment to pay for the conservation and sustainable management of game species. Since its passage more than 70 years ago, this mechanism has provided more than $2 billion of **funding** for conservation.

(25) In the 1970s and 1980s, both Republican and Democratic presidents, working closely with Congress, established landmark laws that provided money for the regulation of toxic chemicals, the cleanup of hazardous waste sites, the construction of sewage treatment plants, and the control of nonpoint source runoff. (Runoff pollution occurs when rain or irrigation water flowing over hard surfaces or loose soil picks up pollutants and deposits them into the nearest lake, creek, estuary,* or groundwater supply.) Additional measures forced polluting industries to invest billions to pay for control technologies designed to reduce air and water pollution. These actions have directly benefited wildlife populations. In several cases, such as that of the American bald eagle and the wood duck, the combined effect of decades of conservation policy **initiatives** has allowed some wildlife populations to rebound to much healthier levels in recent years.

***estuary:** the location where a river connects to a sea

(26) In the mid-1980s, Congress agreed to invest additional resources in new Farm Bill conservation programs such as the Conservation Reserve Program and the Wetlands Reserve Program, which pay farmers and ranchers to conserve habitat and prevent **erosion.** Alongside Farm Bill measures, additional billions

have been spent to protect wetlands and upland bird habitats on private lands by non-profit groups like Ducks Unlimited and Pheasants Forever, often working in partnership with state governments and federal agencies such as the Department of Agriculture and the Fish and Wildlife Service.

(27) Furthermore, the donation of billions of dollars worth of conservation easements* has been encouraged through the federal tax code as well as through the purchase of development rights under the Farm Bill's Farm and Ranchland Protection Program. Groups like the Rocky Mountain Elk Foundation and land trusts across the country have **ensured** that conservation easements will continue to protect millions of acres of valuable open space and wildlife habitat. Such mechanisms are an essential part of American national conservation efforts. Without the **commitment** of such substantial financial resources, a great many farms, ranches, and other opens spaces that provide critical wildlife habitat would be susceptible to economic pressures and risk being developed into yet more strip malls and clusters of oversized houses.

*__easements:__ rights held by property owners to use the land for another purpose

(28) Recent decades have also witnessed the emergence of private companies, **funded** with private capital, that have made the **restoration** of ecosystem health an important part of their business. Sustainably managed forests and smart growth–oriented developments across the land offer tangible evidence that their efforts are having a substantial impact.

(29) The history of conservation in America has shown that where the public recognizes a good cause, it can marshal the political will, the nonprofit passion, and the **corporate** focus to **fund** the work in a relatively straightforward way. But as times change, our **funding** methods can, and need, to change. While many investments in conservation continue to be well justified and will produce public benefits long into the future, record-setting annual federal deficits and accumulated national debts over time

have put intense pressure on conservation budgets at the local, state, and federal levels. . . .

(30) Conservationists, many practiced at the art of raising money, now recognize that new and creative ways to **fund** conservation agendas will need to be identified. . . . Where is, and where will be, the money to **fund** conservation **initiatives** in coming decades?

(31) For instance, . . . the Farm Bill provides billions in crop subsidies and farm-based conservation. The Water Resources Development Act and the Transportation Bill provide hundreds of billions for water projects and building roads and mass transit systems. These pieces of legislation provide billions in tax cuts, and all remain popular bills that are easily and regularly enacted and re-authorized. The challenge is to recognize the **potential** of these and similar large bills to **fund** new conservation work. Developing strategies that convince lawmakers that making conservation investments in the context of these bills is appropriate and necessary is a worthy goal. . . .

(32) **Complementing** these **potential** sources of public-sector **funding** are important sources of non-profit and private-sector conservation financing. Such sources provide capital for a variety of **initiatives,** including: limited development projects; the protection of working farms, ranches, and forests; and the establishment of new markets for ecosystem services such as water purification and air emissions reductions.

(33) In sum, there is no shortage of creative proposals to **fund** the enormous conservation challenges that exist today and that will emerge tomorrow. Many focus on the unconventional use of large **funding** sources that have primarily nonconservation purposes. As the need grows and constraints on the federal budget grow tighter and tighter, conservationists will necessarily have to look to creative ways to **fund** worthy endeavors.

Comprehension Check

Did you understand the readings? Mark these sentences true (T) or false (F).

_____ 1. Yellowstone was the world's first national park.

_____ 2. Hoover Dam is an example of an historic site regulated by the National Park Service.

_____ 3. The size of the national park system has doubled since the year 2000.

_____ 4. In the mid-19th century, early conservation initiatives were a response to the damage done by commercial fishermen.

_____ 5. Most Americans do not favor imposing restrictions on the use of land, water, fish, and game.

_____ 6. Historically, the money to pay for conservation efforts has come from public, private, and philanthropic sources.

_____ 7. One way in which the U.S. government finances the cost of conservation is through taxes on hunting and fishing equipment.

_____ 8. Wildlife populations have benefited from laws passed in the 1970s and 1980s that provided for the control and regulation of sewage and pollution.

_____ 9. Today, the greatest challenge to conservation efforts is Americans' lack of political will.

_____ 10. A "creative" way to pay for conservation is for Congress to combine conservation funding with funding for other large projects such as mass transit.

Word Study

Target Vocabulary

adequate
commit (commitment)
complement
corporate
ensure
erode (erosion)
expand (expansion)
fund
impose
initiate (initiative)
potential
precede (precedent)
range (ranger)
restore
restrain

Word Parts

Exercise 1: Prefixes

Study this sentence from Reading 2.

> . . . simple conservation philosophy, based on the belief that we Americans need to constructively restrain ourselves to **ensure** that resources like game animals will be available for future generations. . . .

In some transitive verbs, the Latin prefix *en-* [or *em-* before a /b/ or /p/] means "cause to be, make" or "put in or on." Thus, *ensure* means "to make sure." Look at the way the underlined words are used in the sentences. Then write a definition for each.

1. This closet is too small. I'm going to hire a carpenter to enlarge it.

   ____

2. The United States Constitution empowers citizens of each state to vote for their own representatives.

   ____

3. Congress enacted a law forbidding oil companies from drilling inside national parks.

   ____

4. The lions encircled the wounded zebra.

   ____

5. They enlarged their house by adding two more rooms.

   ____

What other words can you think of with the *en-* prefix?

Exercise 2: Prefix Review

The prefix *con-*, meaning "together" or "with," has several pronunciations, depending on the sound that begins the second syllable. Study the words. Then complete the statements. Note there is an exception to the rule—the word *corporation*.

commit	**colleague**	**correspond**	**cooperate**	**conservation**
complement	**collect**	**correlate**	**coordinate**	**conduct**
combination				**conversation**
				contemporary

1. We usually use the prefix *com-* before the letters ____, ____, and ____.
2. We usually use the prefix *col-* before the letter ____.
3. We usually use the prefix *cor-* before the letter ____.
4. We usually use the prefix *co-* before the letter ____.
5. We use the prefix *con-* in all other cases.

Can you think of other words beginning with each form of the prefix?

com-	*col-*	*cor-*	*co-*
________	________	________	________
________	________	________	________
________	________	________	________

Exercise 3: Roots

Many English words are built on the Latin root *-cede-*, meaning "go." Study the examples. Analyze the prefixes and suffixes, and discuss the possible meaning of each word. Then use the words to fill in the blanks in the sentences.

antecedent	**exceed**	**precedent**	**recedes**
concede	**intercession**	**procedure**	**succeeded**

1. It is against the law to ________________ the speed limit.

2. Tomorrow I'm going to have a minor surgical ________________.

3. I ________________ that your argument is more logical than mine.

4. It's dangerous to swim during high tide. Let's wait until the tide ________________.

5. Whenever you write the word *this,* make sure it has an ________________.

6. Which king ________________ Louis IV of France?

7. The workers' strike was resolved without the ________________ of the president.

8. There was no historical ________________ for the court's surprising decision.

Word Relationships

Exercise 4: Nouns with *Wild*

Study the nouns with *wild*. Then use the words to complete the sentences.

Noun *wildlife, wildfire, wildflower, wildlands, wilderness*

1. Poppies, which are native to California, are a variety of _______________ .

2. The ________________ spread so quickly that homeowners barely had time to evacuate to safety.

3. Black bears, mountain lions, rainbow trout, and coyotes are just a few of the many species of ________________ found in Yosemite National Park.

4. Many remote Alaskan ________________ can be reached only by air.

5. We took a course in ________________ survival training before we left for our two-week camping trip in the Sierra mountains.

Exercise 5 : Commonly Confused Words

Each pair of words is easily confused. Look up the words in a dictionary. Then fill in the blanks in the sentences with the correct word. Add an *-s* or *-ed* ending as needed.

ensure / insure **complement / compliment** **precede / proceed**

1. My grandmother gave me a beautiful antique necklace. I plan to ________________ it in case it's lost or stolen.

2. Thunder always ________________ lightning.

3. Raita, a kind of yogurt sauce, is an excellent ________________ for spicy Indian food.

4. The aim of the American conservation movement has always been to ________________ that park lands, game animals, and historic sites will be available for future generations to enjoy.

5. The shy student's face lit up when the teacher ________________ her on her composition.

6. Even though several committee members are not here, we must ________________ with our meeting.

The Grammar of Words and Word Families

Exercise 6: Word Families

Use these words to fill in the word family chart. Some words will be used more than once.

<u>adequate</u>	<u>commit</u>	<u>complement (2x)</u>	<u>corporate</u>
adequacy	commitable	complementary	corporately
adequately	commitment		corporateness
			corporation
			corporative
<u>ensure</u>	<u>erode</u>	<u>expand</u>	<u>fund (2x)</u>
ensurer	erodibility	expandability	fundable
	erodible	expandable	funder
	erosion	expansion	funding
<u>impose</u>	<u>initiate (3x)</u>	<u>potential (2x)</u>	<u>precede</u>
imposer	initiation	potentially	precedent
imposing	initiative		precedentless
imposition	initiator		
<u>range (3x)</u>	<u>restore</u>	<u>restrain</u>	
ranger	restorable	restrainability	
	restoration	restrainable	
	restorative	restrained	
	restorer	restraint	

Noun	Noun (person)	Verb	Adjective	Adverb
	—	—	adequate	
	—	commit		—
	—	complement		—
	—		corporate	
—		ensure	—	—
	—	erode		—
	—	expand		—
		fund		—
		impose		—
		initiate		—
	—	—	potential	
	—	precede		—
		range		—
		restore		—
	—	restrain		—

Exercise 7: Word Forms

Complete each sentence with the correct form of the word in parentheses. Add prefixes and suffixes as necessary, and follow spelling rules.

1. (adequate) The man earned enough money to feed and clothe all the members of his family ________________.

2. (erode) The best way to prevent soil ________________ is to plant trees.

3. (range) The store sells plants in a variety of sizes, ________________ from tiny cactuses to huge trees.

4. (restore) Most of the money for the ________________ of the wetlands was donated by private citizens.

5. (restrain) Even if you are angry at your boss, you must show ________________ when you speak to him.

6. (fund) Where is the ________________ for this project going to come from?

7. (initiate) The high-school students showed ________________ when they organized and carried out a carwash to raise money for the homeless.

Exercise 8: Adjective Forms

The *-ed* and *-ing* forms of verbs can function as adjectives. In noun phrases, for example, words with *-ed* or *-ing* endings serve as adjectives—for example, *a disappointing movie, an unwashed plate, a passing grade*. Match the participles on the left with the nouns on the right. Write the phrases on the lines. Some items have more than one answer.

committed	relationship
expanding	building
imposing	step
preceding	economy
restored	speech
restrained	statue

1. ______________________________

2. ______________________________

3. ______________________________

4. ______________________________

5. ______________________________

6. ______________________________

Understanding Words in Context

Exercise 9: Words with Multiple Meanings

Read some of the meanings of the word *range*. Then write the letter and number of the definition that matches the way *range* is used in the sentences.

a. *range* n. 1. the variety of things belonging to the same category: *a wide range of colors.* 2. a category defined by an upper and a lower limit: *the age range from 13 to 18.* 3. the farthest distance that something can travel or function: *a missile range of 25 miles.* 4. a large area of grassy open land 5. a series of hills or mountains

b. *range* v. 1. to vary between a particular upper and lower limit: *The fruit ranged between two and five inches in size.* 2. to move freely around or across an area: 3. to live or grow in a particular geographic area

_____ 1. Buffalo used to range for more than a thousand miles between the Appalachian and Rocky Mountains.

_____ 2. This car has a range of 350 miles on one tank of gas.

_____ 3. Her emotions ranged from euphoria to depression.

_____ 4. The valley was between two ranges of mountains.

_____ 5. The children ranged in age from 3 to 5.

_____ 6. Most of the land that used to be open range has been sold and fenced off.

Exercise 10: Word Meanings in Context

Read the passages from the readings. Then answer the questions.

Passage 1

"Congress followed the Yellowstone precedent with other national parks in the 1890s and early 1900s, including Sequoia, Yosemite, Mount Rainier, Crater Lake, and Glacier. The idealistic impulse to preserve nature was often joined by the pragmatic desire to promote tourism: Western railroads lobbied for many of the early parks and built grand rustic hotels in them to boost their passenger business."

1. According to the passage, the desire to promote tourism was
   a. foolish
   b. practical
   c. a dream
   d. outdated

2. What did the Western railroads do?
   a. build hotels with beautiful lobbies
   b. build parks
   c. try to influence politicians
   d. lose most of their passenger business

Passage 2

"Among several conservation-related initiatives of the era, one of the most important was the effort mounted by sportsmen, in response to the ravages of commercial hunting, to establish seasons and limits as well as formal means of enforcing such restrictions. Their aim, concisely stated, was to sustainably manage wild game. That simple conservation philosophy, based on the belief that we Americans need to constructively restrain ourselves to ensure that resources like game animals will be available for future generations."

3. "Formal means of enforcing such restrictions" could include

   a. park rangers

   b. laws to set seasons and limits

   c. fences and gates to mark off hunting areas

   d. all of the above

4. In this paragraph, the word *game* means

   a. a competitive activity

   b. a sport

   c. animals to be hunted

   d. gambling

Passage 3

"In several cases, such as that of the American bald eagle and the wood duck, the combined effect of decades of conservation policy initiatives has allowed some wildlife populations to rebound to much more healthy levels in recent years."

5. According to the passage, some wildlife populations have

   a. died out

   b. migrated

   c. become sick

   d. come back

Passage 4

"Recent decades have also witnessed the emergence of private companies, funded with private capital, that have made the restoration of ecosystem health an important part of their business. Sustainably managed forests and smart-growth-oriented developments across the land offer tangible evidence that their efforts are having a substantial impact."

6. *Capital* means

   a. money for investment

   b. the city where a country's government is located

   c. a building

   d. a letter used at the beginning of a sentence

7. We can conclude that the efforts of private companies

   a. are difficult to see

   b. are smart

   c. have had little impact

   d. have been successful

Passage 5

"In the mid-1980s, Congress agreed to invest additional resources in new Farm Bill conservation programs such as the Conservation Reserve Program and the Wetlands Reserve Program, which pay farmers and ranchers to conserve habitat and prevent erosion."

8. *Additional resources* probably means

   a. money

   b. land

   c. manpower

   d. time

9. In this context, a *bill* is

   a. a proposed law

   b. money that one must pay

   c. a contract

   d. an advertisement

Using Words in Communication

Exercise 11: Reading

Go the National Park Service website at www.nps.gov. Select a national park, and read about it. Find the answers to these questions.

1. What is the name of the park? Where is it located? How big is it?
2. What is the history of the park?
3. What are the special characteristics or features of the park?
4. How many tourists visit the park each year?
5. What special conservation and environmental challenges does the park face? What conservation efforts, if any, are underway?

Exercise 12: Writing

Using the answers to the questions, write a 2–4 page report about the national park you selected. If possible, include photos of the park you selected. Share your report with your classmates.

Exercise 13: Reading and Speaking

Research the 1944 explosion at the Port Chicago Naval Magazine or the events behind another historical site/monument. Why should it be remembered? What should everyone know about what happened? Prepare a 5–7 minute oral report about the site.

Exercise 14: Critical Thinking

These questions will help you develop your critical-thinking skills. Critical thinking helps you evaluate information and reach good conclusions using the information that is given. Ask yourself the questions as you work on your answers: What information in the reading supports my answer? What other information do I have to support my conclusion? Where can I get more information about the topic?

The reading presents an ethical case study. Read it. After you read, discuss the questions in groups.

Should private oil companies be allowed to explore or drill for oil in national parks or wilderness areas—both on land and under the sea—that historically have been protected by the federal government? That is a question that the U.S. Congress has been debating for many years.

People who oppose oil exploration in protected areas offer these arguments in support of their position:

1. No matter how much oil is discovered in places such as the Alaska National Wildlife Refuge, our need for oil will always grow more quickly than our ability to extract it from the ground. Therefore, conservation (such as increasing fuel efficiency of cars) and use of non-polluting alternative fuels are the only true long-term solutions to our dependence on oil.
2. Drilling for oil, and transporting extracted oil to distant refineries, disrupts the feeding, mating, and migration patterns of native animals and fish.
3. The machinery used to drill for and transport oil, plus the housing, sewage facilities, roads, etc. that would be needed by oil workers, spoils the unique natural beauty of previously untouched wilderness areas.

In response, proponents of oil exploration make these arguments:

1. The U.S. must reduce its dependence on oil imported from foreign countries with unstable governments.

2. The U.S. has the safest and most secure oil-drilling equipment in the world. During hurricanes Katrina and Rita, as an example, oil platforms in the Caribbean were not damaged at all.

3. In some wilderness areas where drilling has been allowed, such as Prudhoe Bay in Alaska, the size of caribou herds has actually increased in recent years.

4. Alternative fuels that do not harm the environment are years away from being readily available and practical to use. Biofuels, for example, have harmed rather than helped the environment as a result of farmers cutting down trees in tropical areas in order to plant soybeans or sugar cane.

Sometimes there is a moratorium on oil exploration in protected areas. Other times drilling is allowed. The issue is constantly being debated in Congress and will certainly come up for a vote again soon.

1. Based on the arguments presented here, do you believe the U.S. Congress should allow oil drilling in protected wilderness areas? Why or why not?

2. If you support drilling, do you believe there should be any restrictions on the companies that receive drilling contracts?

3. If you oppose drilling, can you think of any present or future circumstances under which you would allow drilling?

4. In order to reduce our dependence on oil, whether domestic or foreign, what you can do to decrease your use of energy?

Appendix 1
Academic Word List

This list, compiled by Coxhead (2000), contains 570 word familes that are important for students to know to read texts and do well in academic settings. Words explicitly studied in this text as target words are set in bold and marked by the numbers of the units in which they appear (target unit number is in bold). Words that are not studied explicitly but occur in the text are set in ordinary type and marked by the number of the unit in which they appear. Words studied as target words in *Vocabulary Mastery 1* are shown with an asterisk. Words studied as target words in *Vocabulary Mastery 2* are shown with underlining.

abandon Unit 2
<u>abstract</u> Unit 1
academy
access Units 2, 5
accommodate* Unit 6
accompany Unit 3
accumulate* Unit 6
accurate Unit 2
achieve Units **1,** 4, 6
acknowledge Unit 2
acquire* Units 5, 6
<u>adapt</u> Units 1, 5
adequate Units 5, **6**
adjacent Unit 1
<u>adjust</u>
administrate Unit 2
<u>adult</u> Unit 4
advocate
affect Unit 5
aggregate
aid
albeit
allocate
alter
<u>alternative</u>
ambiguous
<u>amend</u>
analogy
analyse (analyze) Units **2,** 5
annual Units 4, 5, 6
anticipate
apparent Unit 1
append
appreciate
<u>approach</u> Unit 3
appropriate* Units 5, 6
approximate Unit 3
arbitrary
area Units 3, 5, 6
aspect Unit 1
<u>assemble</u>
assess Unit 5
<u>assign</u> Unit 4
assist Unit 1
<u>assume</u> Units 1, 3, 6
assure
attach
attain Unit 3
attitude
attribute Unit 3
author Unit 4
authority* Units 2, 4, 6
automate* Unit 3
available Units 5, 6
<u>aware</u> Units 1, 3, 5
behalf
benefit* Units 3, 6
bias Unit 2
bond
brief* Unit 4
bulk
capable*
<u>capacity</u> Units 1, 6
category
cease Unit 1
challenge* Units 2, 3, 4, 5, 6
channel
chapter
chart
chemical* Units 5, 6
<u>circumstance</u> Unit 2
cite
<u>civil</u> Units 4, 5, 6

clarify
classic Unit 4
clause
code Unit 6
coherent
coincide
collapse Unit 3
colleague Unit 2
commence
comment
commission
commit Unit 6
commodity
communicate*
community Unit 4
compatible
compensate
compile
complement Unit 6
complex Units 2, **5**
component
compound
comprehensive
comprise Unit 6
compute
conceive
concentrate Units 3, 5
concept* Units 1, 6
conclude Units 2, 4
concurrent
conduct Unit 4
confer Unit 2
confine
confirm
conflict*
conform Unit 4
consent
consequent Unit 2
considerable
consist Units 2, **3,** 6
constant Unit 1
constitute Unit 2
constrain Unit 6
construct* Units 1, 6
consult
consume*
contact*
contemporary
context* Unit 6
contract* Unit 3
contradict
contrary Unit 1
contrast
contribute Units 2, 5
controversy* Unit 4
convene Units 1, 6
converse
convert
convince Units 3, 6
cooperate Units **3,** 4
coordinate*
core
corporate Unit 6
correspond
couple Unit 1
create* Units 1, 4, 5, 6
credit Unit 6
criteria Unit 2
crucial
culture Units 4, 6
currency
cycle
data*
debate Unit 4
decade* Units 2, 4, 5, 6
decline Unit 5
deduce
define* Units 5, 6
definite Unit 3
demonstrate Unit 4
denote
deny Units 2, 3, 4
depress* Unit 4
derive
design Units 1, 6
despite Units 3, 4
detect Unit 5
deviate Unit 2
device
devote Units 3, 4
differentiate
dimension
diminish
discrete
discriminate
displace
display
dispose
distinct Units 2, 3, 4
distort Unit 1
distribute
diverse
document* Units 2, 3
domain Unit 1
domestic Unit 2
dominate*
draft Unit 2
drama Units 1, 2, 4
duration Unit 5
dynamic Unit 5
economy* Unit 6
edit Units 2, 4
element*
eliminate

emerge* Units 5, 6
emphasis Unit 1
empirical
enable
encounter Unit 2
energy* Unit 3
enforce Unit 6
enhance
enormous Unit 6
ensure Units 2, **6**
entity Unit 3
environment*
equate
equip* Unit 6
equivalent Unit 2
erode Unit 6
error
establish* Units 2, 6
estate
estimate* Unit 5
ethic Units 2, 6
ethnic
evaluate Unit 2
eventual Units 1, 3, 4
evident* Units 1, 2, 6
evolve* Unit 5
exceed Unit 3
exclude*
exhibit
expand Units 3, **6**
expert Unit 5
explicit
exploit Unit 6
export
expose Units 4, **5**
external Unit 3
extract
facilitate Units **5,** 6

factor* Units 4, 5
feature Unit 1
federal Unit 6
fee
file
final* Units 2, 4, 5
finance* Units 2, 6
finite
flexible
fluctuate Unit 5
focus Units 2, 3, 5, 6
format
formula
forthcoming
foundation Units **1,** 6
found Units 1, 2, 3, 4, 5, 6
framework
function*
fund Units 2, 5, **6**
fundamental Unit 4
furthermore
gender
generate*
generation Units **1,** 4, 6
globe*
goal* Unit 3, 5, 6
grade
grant Unit 4
guarantee
guideline
hence
hierarchy Unit 2
highlight
hypothesis
identical Unit 2
identify* Units 5, 6
ideology
ignorance Unit 4

illustrate Unit 4
image* Unit 2
immigrate
impact Units 2, 4, 6
implement* Unit 5
implicate Unit 4
implicit
imply
impose Unit 6
incentive
incidence Units 2, **5**
incline Unit 3
income*
incorporate
index
indicate Units 3, 5
individual*
induce
inevitable Unit 3
infer
infrastructure Units **1,** 5
inherent Unit 4
inhibit
initial
initiate Unit 6
injure
innovate Unit 1
input
insert
insight Units 2, **4**
inspect Unit 1
instance Units 3, 6
institute Units **2,** 6
instruct Unit 2
integral
integrate
integrity Unit 2
intelligence

intense Units 1, 2, 3, 4, 6
interact Unit 4
intermediate
internal
interpret
interval Unit 2
intervene Unit 4
intrinsic
invest* Units 5, 6
investigate Unit 2
invoke
involve Units 4, 6
isolate
issue* Units 3, 4, 5
item
job Units 2, 3
journal Unit 2
justify Units 1, 6
label Units 2, 4, 5
labor*
layer Unit 3
lecture
legal* Unit 6
legislate Unit 6
levy
liberal
licence (license)
likewise
link Unit 6
locate* Unit 1
logic Unit 3
maintain Units 1, 2, **3,** 4, 6
major Units 1, 2, 4, **5**
manipulate
manual
margin*
mature
maximise (maximize)
Units **3,** 6
mechanism Units 3, 6
media Unit 4
mediate
medical Unit 5
medium
mental Unit 3
method Units **2,** 3, 4, 5, 6
migrate Unit 3
military* Unit 6
minimal Unit 6
minimise (minimize)
minimum
ministry
minor Unit 1
mode
modify Unit 1
monitor* Unit 5
motive Unit 2
mutual
negate
network
neutral
nevertheless Unit 1
nonetheless
norm
normal* Units 1, 2, 3, 4, 5
notion
notwithstanding
nuclear*
objective*
obtain* Unit 2
obvious Unit 2
occupy*
occur Units 2, 5, 6
odd
offset
ongoing
option
orient Unit 6
outcome Units **2,** 3
output
overall
overlap
overseas
panel
paradigm
paragraph
parallel
parameter Unit 3
participate* Unit 3
partner Unit 6
passive*
perceive Units 2, 3
percent* Units 4, 5
period Unit 2
persist Unit 5
perspective Unit 6
phase
phenomenon
philosophy Units **1,** 3, 6
physical* Unit 3
plus
policy Units 2, 4, 6
portion
pose Unit 5
positive Units 2, 5
potential Unit 6
practitioner
precede Unit 6
precise Units 1, 3
predict Unit 5
predominant
preliminary
presume
previous Units 1, 2, 5
primary Unit 6
prime
principal

principle Unit 2
prior
priority
proceed
process* Unit 3
professional* Unit 5
prohibit*
project Units 1, 6
promote Units 4, 6
proportion Unit 5
prospect Unit 1
protocol
psychology
publication Unit 6
publish Units 2, **4**
purchase* Unit 6
pursue* Unit 3
qualitative
quote
radical
random
range Units 2, **6**
ratio
rational
react Unit 5
recover*
refine
regime
region Units 1, 5, 6
register*
regulate* Unit 6
reinforce
reject Unit 2
relax
release Unit 2
relevant
reluctance
rely Units
remove Unit 4

require Units 5, 6
research Unit 4
reside Unit 4
resolve
resource* Units 2, 6
respond Units 4, 5, 6
restore Unit 4, **6**
restrain Unit 6
restrict* Unit 6
retain Unit 1
reveal Unit 2
revenue
reverse* Unit 1
revise
revolution Units 3, 6
rigid
role Unit 2
route Unit 3
scenario
schedule
scheme
scope
section Units 1, 6
sector Unit 6
secure Units 2, 5, 6
seek Unit 4
select
sequence
series Unit 1
sex Unit 5
shift Unit 5
significant* Units 1, 3, 5, 6
similar Units 2, 3, 6
simulate*
site Units 1, 6
so-called
sole Unit 3
somewhat
source* Units 2, 4, 6

specific
specify
sphere
stable Units 1, 5
statistic
status Unit 3
straightforward Units 4, 6
strategy Units 5, 6
stress Unit 5
structure Unit 1
style Unit 1
submit
subordinate
subsequent Unit 6
subsidy Unit 6
substitute
successor
sufficient* Units 1, 5
sum
summary Unit 4
supplement Unit 5
survey Units 3, **4,** 6
survive* Units 1, 2, 3, 6
suspend
sustain* Units 1, 4, 6
symbol
tape Units 2, 5
target Units **4,** 5
task*
team
technique Unit 5
technology* Units 5, 6
temporary Unit 3
tense
terminate
text Units 2, 4
theme Units 1, **4**
theory
thereby

thesis Unit 2
topic
trace
tradition
transfer
<u>transform</u> Units 2, 3
transit Unit 6
transmit Unit 3
transport Units 1, 6
trend
trigger
<u>ultimate</u> Units 2, 3, 6
undergo
underlie
undertake Unit 2
uniform
unify
unique* Unit 1
utilize Units 1, 6
valid
<u>vary</u> Unit 1
vehicle
version
via
violate
virtual Units 2, 4
visible Units 1, **3**
<u>vision</u> Units 3, 6
<u>visual</u>
volume*
voluntary Unit 6
welfare*
whereas
whereby
widespread

Appendix 2
Expansion Activities

Unit 1: Architecture (pages xiv–27)

Frank Lloyd Wright

1. Study "A Virtual Look at Frank Lloyd Wright" at www.delmars.com/wright/index.html. Which of Wright's designs not studied in the textbook do you like best? From which period is it from? What do you like about it? Talk about your choice in a small group.
2. Watch *Frank Lloyd Wright: A Film by Ken Burns & Lynn Novick* available from the PBS store (www.pbs.org/flw). Or search local listings to see when it might be on television.
3. Frank Lloyd Wright started his own architecture school housed at Taliesin. If you were to start a school in your field, what would it be?

Architecture

1. Work with a small group and imagine you are a team of architects commissioned to design a hotel. Prepare to present your hotel's name, location, structure, and features to the rest of the class in a 10-minute group presentation.
2. Research things that affect a building's strength and survival during an earthquake. What foundation and infrastructure materials and designs would you use if you lived in an earthquake-prone area such as California in the United States?
3. Think of a unique building or structure that you like and one that you don't. Find pictures. Be prepared to talk about what you like and don't like with a small group.

Unit 2: Watergate (pages 28–59)

Watergate

1. The Watergate scandal began with five men breaking into the Democratic National Committee headquarters in Washington, DC, and ended with the resignation of President Richard Nixon. If this happened today, do you think it would end the same way? What might be different?

2. Political cartoons are used by newspaper and magazine editorial cartoonists to send messages to the readers. See the example on page 42. They often use symbolism and exaggeration, among other techniques, to get their point across. Search the Internet for political cartoons published during and after the Watergate scandal. Share examples with the rest of the class.

Journalism

1. Read *All the President's Men* or watch the film. Talk about how the events depicted affected journalism.
2. During the Watergate years and for many years later, Woodward and Bernstein never revealed who Deep Throat was. Research the laws associated with reporters not revealing sources. Find a story about another journalist who has not revealed his or her source, the circumstances, and any punishments he or she faced.
3. Bring in a political cartoon from a recent newspaper. Prepare to discuss what event or person the cartoon is editorializing.
4. Look at a copy of the school, city, or national newspaper. Which section of the paper do you like to read most? What kind of stories would you like to write if you were a journalist? Talk about your choices with a small group.

Unit 3: Physical Feats (pages 60–89)

Mount Everest and Mountain Climbing

1. Read *Into Thin Air* or watch the film. Think about what happened and what you would have done similarly or differently than the mountaineering team.
2. Find a list of facts about Mount Everest to share with a small group.

Marathons

1. If possible, find a video or news clip about a marathon.
2. Attend a local fun run or walk (usually one mile) or race (often 5K or 10K). Consider walking with your classmates or volunteering to cheer for the runners as they cross the finish line. Be prepared to share your experiences with the class.

4. Work with a partner to research the training required to run a marathon. Develop a program as if you were going to prepare for the marathon in the next Olympics.

Physical Feats

1. Brainstorm a list of physical feats. Then create a list of the dangers associated with each. Prepare a list to share with the class.
2. Discuss the personality traits and physical characteristics of a person who participates in extreme physical feats. What traits do you share? Which do you not have, but wish you did?

Unit 4: *To Kill a Mockingbird* (pages 90–115)

To Kill a Mockingbird

1. Read the novel. Write a book report for class.
2. Watch the film and talk about your own insights gained from the movie.
3. Imagine the class is the jury who must decide the guilt or innocence of Atticus Finch's client. Role-play what the jurors might say after hearing Finch's speech.
4. Talk about the themes of the novel: race and class. Watch Martin Luther King's "I Have a Dream" speech (available on various sites), and review Atticus Finch's speech in the novel. Do you think race and class are still issues in the United States? Be prepared to explain.

Novels

1. What novel would you add to the MLA's list of books all adults should read before they die? Prepare a 1–2 minute oral presentation on the book and why you chose it.
2. Research other Pulitzer Prize–winning novels. Choose one to summarize for the class.

Unit 5: Global Health (pages 116–45)

Tuberculosis

1. Research DOTS. Discuss the pros and cons to this strategy with a small group.
2. Write a report about someone who died from tuberculosis. Lists can be found at various online sites.
3. Tuberculosis has reemerged throughout history and is still present today. Work with a partner to create a timeline of the history of the disease. Compare timelines as a class.

Global Health

1. One way to prevent some illnesses, such as the flu, is to get a shot with the vaccine. Since vaccines are not always available, think about other things people can do to prevent catching colds or the flu. Work with a group to brainstorm a list of prevention methods to share with the class.
2. Research a common disease or illness and compile a list of symptoms. Read the symptoms to the class. Can anyone diagnose the disease you are describing?
3. Watch the movie *Outbreak,* and discuss if you think modern-day society is prepared to handle such a virus.

Unit 6: Conserving Natural Resources (pages 146–76)

National Parks

1. Watch Ken Burns' series *The National Parks: America's Best Idea* on DVD or check local listings at www.pbs.org. Video segments are available at www.pbs.org/nationalparks/.
2. Imagine you get to take a summer vacation with three classmates. Research America's national parks and choose one for your trip. Start by visiting the National Park Service's website at www.nps.gov/index.htm. Prepare a presentation that includes the reason for your choice and the activities you will participate in on your vacation.
3. The National Park Service employs more than 20,000 people in a variety of roles. A partial list is available at www.nps.gov/aboutus/workwithus.htm. Prepare a 1–2 minute oral presentation on which job you'd like to have as a summer internship and why.

National Resources

1. Compile a list of reasons why nature should be preserved, and prepare a presentation to a group of wealthy investors persuading them to invest in natural resources rather than urban development. Include your plans for the area.
2. Explore a local park. Create a list of benefits the park has to offer, and share those with the class.